10 Ways To Survive A Valley Experience

HARRIETT JONES

10 Ways To Survive A Valley Experience

HARRIETT JONES

T&J Publishers
A Small Independent Publisher
with a Big Voice

Printed in the United States of America
by T&J Publishers (Atlanta, GA.)
www.TandJPublishers.com

© Copyright 2015 by Harriett Jones

Unauthorized duplication is prohibited by law. All rights in this book are reserved. No part of this book may be used or reproduced in any manner whatsoever without expressed, written permission from the author.

All Bible verses used are from the New King James Version (1982) by Thomas Nelson, Inc., and the King James Version (1987). Also used: Dictonary.com (definitions of valley 4, 5) retrieved 1/2/2015 from: http:dictionary.reference.com/brose/valley.

Cover design by Timothy Flemming, Jr.
Book format and layout by Timothy Flemming, Jr.

ISBN: 978-0-9962165-8-6

To contact author, send email to:
Jonesgirl172@yahoo.com

DEDICATIONS

First and foremost, I thank God for Him allowing me to go through personal valley experiences and now being able to write this book *10 Ways to Survive A Valley Experience*. With God's love, grace, and mercy I can withstand any trial and come out praising God. God is the mastermind and architect of the book and by His Holy Spirit I was able to write the things He revealed to me.

Also I want to thank my family and church family for their prayers and support.

Special thanks to my pastor Rev. Cleon Warren, Sr. (St. John Missionary Baptist Church, Homer, La) and Rev. Willie Johnson (Mt. Superior Missionary Baptist Church, Homer); for you all showed me to believe in God, Jesus the Christ, and the Holy Spirit—my Teacher. I love you all.

"Yea, though I walk through the valley of the shadow of death, I will fear no evil: for thou art with me; thy rod and thy staff they comfort me."—Psalm 23:4

TABLE OF CONTENTS

INTRODUCTION: A Valley Experience   11

CHAPTER 1: Key 1: God First   25

CHAPTER 2: Key 2: Look Up   39

CHAPTER 3: Key 3: Don't Walk Away   53

CHAPTER 4: Key 4: Get Shelter   67

CHAPTER 5: Key 5: Get The Word   79

CHAPTER 6: Key 6: Praise Your Way Through   93

CHAPTER 7: Key 7: Pray   103

CHAPTER 8: Key 8: Speak Success   119

CHAPTER 9: Key 9: Learn To Love   133

CHAPTER 10: Key 10: God First And Last   165

CHAPTER 11: Exaltation: He Brought Me Out Alright   187

Introduction

A VALLEY EXPERIENCE

"For I consider that the sufferings of this present time are not worthy to be compared with the glory which shall be revealed in us."—Romans 8:18, NKJV

For some people, the valley experience is not imaginary; IT IS REAL. Horrible circumstances, issues, sicknesses and troubles cause heartaches and pains. A valley is "a low point or interval in any process, representation, or situation; any place, period, or situation that is filled with fear, gloom, foreboding, or the like (i.e. the valley of despair" (dictionary.com). A valley experience can also include depression, fatigue, hatred, danger, anger, and disappointments. There are three positions in life—either you are going through the valley, coming out the valley, or you're about to go into a valley—and valley experiences happen to us all. Things may be terrible, but there is still HOPE. The only hope in surviving a valley experience is GOD.

There are many types of valley experiences. Here are

10 Ways To Survive A Valley Experience

a few of them:

- Physical
- Family/Social
- Financial
- Sexual
- Mental
- Emotional
- Spiritual

As we dig deeper into these experiences, you'll discover the solutions to each one of them.

PHYSICAL VALLEY EXPERIENCES

Physical valley experiences consist of things that attack our physical bodies. Sicknesses such as bacterial infections, virus, high blood pressure, arthritis, etc. can wreak havoc in our bodies, making us grow weak, weary, and giving us terrible symptoms such as pain, vomiting, headaches, cramps, and other signs. Diseases can attack the body and debilitate an individual. Cancers, diabetes, AIDS, lupus, asthma, Alzheimer's, strokes, and Multiple Sclerosis can kill us. No one wants to hear a doctor tell him or her that they have a life threatening disease, but it happens every day.

We do not understand the causes behind every sickness and disease, nor have the cures for them, but God is a healer. God heals supernaturally as well as naturally through medications. To tap into God's healing power a person must believe that God can heal ALL sickness and disease.

Also, in the physical valley experience, there are harmful things that we put into our bodies such as drugs and alcohol. Drug and alcohol addictions destroy vital or-

Introduction: A Valley Experience

gans such as our brain cells, our livers, the pancreas, and our heart. The misuse of both prescription and illegal drugs can cause all kind of pains. Often people use drugs and alcohol to numb other types of pain they are having, but drugs and alcohol abuse only leads to more experiences such as sickness, imprisonment and mental problems. If left untreated, alcoholism and drug abuse can even be fatal.

The cure to alcohol and drug addiction is substitution. Do not substitute alcohol and drugs with other harmful activities such as smoking or overeating; substitute the bad things with God's word. Quench your thirsty soul with reading the Bible, prayer, and worship. Ask God to remove the desire for drugs and the taste for alcohol from your mouth. God can detox you and fill you with His Holy Spirit. God will help you resist the urge to binge on drugs and alcohol.

FAMILY/ SOCIAL VALLEY EXPERIENCES

Family and social valley experiences are things that cause disorder in the family and/or community. Jealousy, hatred, and disrespect causes many disagreements that lead to family feuds—the husband can be against the wife, the wife against the husband, and children against their parents. In a family/social valley experience you can go through tragic events such as a divorce, the loss of a parent, the loss of a child, a fire, a flood, have to deal with sick or ill family members, experience a job loss, or a broken home.

Many families and societies are in turmoil because few people desire to have loving relationships. Selfishness, pride, Satan, and sin can tear a family or society apart. When the devil attacks the family (and he does), he is attacking God because God created family. Also, you can be in a family/social valley experience when communities are divided due to race and socioeconomic status. Blacks, Whites, Latinos, Asians, Hispanics, Chinese, and many other ethnic groups call America home. The social family must stop killing one another.

The solution to the survival of family/social valley experiences is God. God can unite. The family/society must turn to God so that the Earth will be prosperous. Each individual must have a mindset to humble him/herself and do what God says is right. God says love one another, forgive, work in unity, and be fruitful and multiply. Divided we fall, but united we shall stand.

Domestic abuse is another type of family/social valley experience in which violence is inflicted on women and men. Living in an abusive marriage is a nightmare. If your husband or wife is physically kicking, hitting, punching, slapping, burning, dragging, choking, fighting, or hurting you in any way, please get help. No one deserves to be physically attacked or abused in any way. First, pray to God for the person's mind and behavior to change. Next, seek out a pastor, marriage counselor, or therapist who can talk to you about Godly relationships, anger management, duties in a marriage and communication skills. Use words to communicate with your spouse, not your hands, feet, and fists. Have law enforcement personnel get involved if you think the situation is out of control or the abuse is getting worse. We're supposed to love and forgive, but we don't have to tolerate abuse. God can change the abuser, but the abuser must be willing to change. A lot of women and men don't want to report their abusers, and they often go through in silence. Abuse isn't a joke, it isn't normal, nor is it Godly. Sometimes, dysfunction may appear normal if a victim has

Introduction: A Valley Experience

a family history of abuse in their childhood. If you've suffered abuse, it's not your fault. We put on masks or facades and pretend that the abuse is our fault or that it's acceptable in one way or another. Thankfully, God knows what you have been through and/or are currently going through, and He has provided you with help both naturally and supernaturally. God can heal families if they make Him their top priority.

Child abuse is another type of family/social valley experience. The Bible instructs parents to discipline their children, but not abuse them. Child abuse can be fatal and it is a crime. There is much debate about spanking or whipping children its impact on their future development. According to the Bible spanking is justified, but God does not intend for children to be abused physically, mentally, emotionally, sexually, verbally, or in any other way. God loves children and they are a blessing from God which should be treated with love, respect, and care. Proverbs 13:24 says, "He who spares his rod hates his son, but he who loves him disciplines him promptly." When children misbehave or disrespect their parents, they should be disciplined. If the rod of correction is used, it should be used in a loving way, and not when the parent is upset or angry. A parent might have to walk away, calm down, pray, and then go back and handle the situation. Children are not to be abused; they're to be reared under the love and admonition of God.

FINANCIAL VALLEY EXPERIENCES

Financial valley experiences are attacks on our finances, jobs and businesses. Poverty is rampant worldwide, and some people lack the daily necessities of life such as food, clothing, shelter, shoes, and water. Also, the love of money is the root of all evil and many will lie, steal, cheat, and kill to get it. I Timothy 6:10 says, " For the love of money is a root of all kinds of evil, for which some have strayed from the faith in their greediness, and pierced themselves through with many sorrows." Greed causes economic ruin and hurts individuals. If people have no income because of sicknesses and disabilities, they will be in financial lows. People who're being laid off, fired from their jobs, and losing their businesses will often find themselves in financial valleys. If people have jobs but still can't pay their bills, or they don't know how to manage and use money wisely, they'll end-up having a valley experience. The solution to financial valley experiences is God. God told us He is our Provider—He'll provide the things that we need. God also told us to bring Him our tithes, give offerings, and share our blessings with others. God's financial plan is better than any financial plan a human can develop.

SEXUAL VALLEY EXPERIENCES

Sexual valley experiences are attacks on sexuality—it is being sexually immoral or perversions. God designed sex specifically for married couples, which in His definition entails one man and one woman. Premarital sex, multiple sexual partners, same sex marriage, and sexual abuse is against God's will. Sex in marriage is un-defiled, but fornicators, adulterers, adulteresses, and whore-mongers will be judged. Television, the internet, and the world has turned sex into a business. Skimpy, revealing clothes; X or R rated movies, sex toys, and pornography can be purchased online and in stores. Young people are bombarded with sexy billboards, commercials, magazine ads, and sexual images on the internet. Satan has perverted what God intended to be special

Introduction: A Valley Experience

for married heterosexual couples, turning it into something immoral and abominable. God help us!

Fornication is sex outside of marriage. When boyfriends and girlfriends have sex without a marriage covenant or live together without being married, they're sinning. Satan has tried to make fornication normal like "everybody's doing it." Satan does not show the dark side of fornication such as unwed mothers, single parent homes, STDs, shame, and guilt. Fornication is sinful and cannot be glamorized by humanity—and everyone is not doing it. Parents should teach their children to remain virgins until marriage. The Bible instructs us to practice abstinance and flee from fornication. God forgives sin, but to obey is better. The solution to fornication is found in 1 Corinthians 6:18: "Flee sexual immorality. Every sin that a man does is outside the body, but he who commits sexual immorality sins against his own body." To resist the temptation to fornicate, escape from every place that you feel weak in, or simply get married.

Adultery is being unfaithful to one's marriage vows. When married people have sex with other partners, it is sin. At the altar you made a covenant to love your spouse and be committed to them until death do you part. Adultery is the cause of broken homes, divorce, and pain. The antidote for adultery is to ask God for forgiveness, ask your spouse for forgiveness, and ask God to create in you a new and clean heart.

Homosexuality is sex between individuals who are the same sex/gender. God said that homosexuality is abomination, unclean and unnatural. Homosexuality is not God's way. Leviticus 18:22 says, "You shall not lie with a male as with a woman. It is an abomination." The solution to homosexuality is God, and being born of a new spirit. Jesus says, "Most assuredly, I say unto you, unless one is born again, he cannot see the kingdom of God" (John 3:3). God is a deliverer.

Sexual abuse is also a misuse of God's creation. Rape, incest, lewdness, bestiality (sex with animals), child molestation, sex trafficking, and prostitution fall into this category. I think there is a demonic spirit behind sexual abuse and sexual immorality. The solution to sexual abuse is found in God. God tells us to be led by the Spirit of God. Apostle Paul says, "For the weapons of our warfare are not carnal, but mighty in God for the pulling down of strongholds, casting down arguments and every high thing that exalts itself against the knowledge of God, bringing every thought into captivity to the obedience of Christ" (2 Corinthians 10:4-5). Put no confidence in the flesh. Put confidence in God.

MENTAL VALLEY EXPERIENCES

Mental valley experiences are attacks against the mind. Psychiatric disorders, mental illnesses, hallucinations, anxiety, and depression can cause an unstable mind. God does not want people to be bound in any way. He wants us to be free to worship Him. The cure to mental valley experiences is God. God is a mind regulator. He works to renew our minds. The Bible says in Isaiah 26:3, "You will keep him in perfect peace, whose mind is stayed on You, because he trusts in You." Mental illness sufferers are in constant fear of bad things happening to them and/or their family members. To combat fears you must learn to walk in love; also, "do not be conformed to this world, but be transformed by the renewing of your mind, that you may prove what is that good and acceptable and perfect will of God" (Romans

Introduction: A Valley Experience

12:2). A Christ-centered mind will end any mental valley experience.

EMOTIONAL VALLEY EXPERIENCES

Emotional valley experiences are attacks against our emotional health. Emotions are feelings, and individuals in an emotional valley experience feelings of unhappiness, worry, sadness, fear, failure, loneliness, panic attacks, disappointment, depression, being un-loved, not being good enough, and hopelessness. Some of the cause for negative emotions are a loss of a parent, loss of a child, death of a relative, tragedy, and trauma. Not only does emotional pain cause grief, but it can also cloud a person's judgment. For instance, a person may have had a healthy diet and lifestyle, but became depressed and began over-eating and/or using drugs; a person may have been faithful to his or her spouse for years, but feeling loneliness led them to commit adultery; but regardless of how low a person feels and how sinful he or she has become, the solution for their survival is still found in God. God comforts, counsels, and fixes broken hearts. Prayer and praise is the antidote for surviving an emotional valley. The cure is to give worry, distress, loneliness, anxiety, stress, depression, and emotional baggage to Jesus and allow Him to see you through the valley. As Joseph Scriven wrote in 1855, "What a friend we have in Jesus":

> What a friend we have in Jesus,
> all our sins and griefs to bear.
> What a privilege to carry
> everything to God in prayer.
> O what peace we often forfeit,
> Oh, what needless pain we bear,

All because we do not carry,
Everything to God in prayer.
Have we trials and temptations?
Is there trouble anywhere?
We should never be discouraged-
Take it to the Lord in prayer.
Can we find a friend so faithful,
who will all our sorrows share?
Jesus knows our every weakness:
Take it to the Lord in prayer.

When we take our emotional issues to Jesus, we will find rest, peace, and stability for our souls.

SPIRITUAL VALLEY EXPERIENCES

Spiritual valley experiences are attacks against our spiritual well-being. We have a mind, body, soul, and a spirit. Christians are saved and have the Spirit of Jesus living inside of them, but they can still experience spiritual valleys. We wish we could be immune from stress, attacks, trials and tests, but God has a plan and everything will work out for our good. Both Christians and non-Christians go through spiritual valley experiences. Spiritual warfare is real, but if we desire to be protected we must run to God.

Unsaved people go through valley experiences. Unsaved people do good things and they do bad things, and they usually live like they want, but bad things happen to them as well; but in their valley experiences they may go to doctors, lawyers, psychiatrists, psychics, witchdoctors, and the world's system for relief. Unsaved people try everything but God. In the end, unsaved people are searching for a living hope that can only be found in Jesus Christ. Fortu-

Introduction: A Valley Experience

nately, God is the Savior and He can save the lost and heal any broken spirit. Romans 5:6 says, "For when we were still without strength, in due time Christ died for the ungodly."

Idol worshipers go through spiritual valley experiences. They worship false gods, themselves, God's creation, cars, homes, children, and money. Idol worship always fails. People must come to Jesus and stop serving idols. God is a jealous God and He wants all of you: spirit, soul, and body. We are created to worship God, and not people, places, or things.

Ignorant people go through spiritual valley experiences. Due to ignorance many people persecute others, blaspheme God, and practice sin. They haven't been taught the way of righteousness, and do not know Jesus; however, they still have a God-given sense of right and wrong that will speak to them no matter how low they fall. There is still hope because if they repent, turn around, and get to know God, they will become knowledgeable and survive.

Demonic possession, influence, and/or oppression also can attack individuals and cause them to go through a spiritual valley experience. Demonic forces can cause people to hurt themselves and others physically, socially, financially, sexually, emotionally, mentally, etc. There is expectation for survival because Satan is a defeated enemy. God will cast out demons and fight our battles. Satan, demons, fallen angels, unclean and evil spirits, devils—they are real. To overcome satanic oppression and possession we must totally submit to God and then plead the blood of Jesus over our spirits, souls, bodies, and families. The enemy wants to destroy the family, health, wealth, people, marriages, churches, communities, and world peace. God is the only defense and offense we have in spiritual warfare. According to Ephesians 6:13-18, the spiritual armor of God includes: truth, the breastplate of righteousness, the gospel of peace, the shield of faith, the helmet of salvation, the sword of the spirit (which is the word of God), and "praying always with all prayer and supplication in the Spirit, being watchful to this end with all perseverance and supplication for all the saints" (verse 18).

Backsliding is also a spiritual valley experience. Backsliders are people who know God, but still go into sin. Backsliders once went to church, got saved, and loved God, but other things, people, and cares took their focus off of God. The hope of survival for a backslider is God. "Return, O backsliding children," says the Lord, "for I am married to you. I will take you, one from a city and two from a family and I will bring you to Zion" (Jeremiah 3:14). God won't leave you, even if you leave Him. Jeremiah 3:22 says, "Return, you backsliding children and I will heal your backslidings." God is a forgiving God and He will accept you back even if you have been unfaithful to Him. Just go to Him.

Christian suffering is also a form of spiritual warfare. To suffer means to undergo pain. Throughout history, men and women have received beatings, imprisonment, persecutions, trials, and have even been killed due to their belief in Jesus Christ. President Abraham Lincoln (1809-1865) was assassinated because he heard from God and was trying to emancipate slaves and end slavery. Lincoln lost his natural life, but his death was not in vain because many years later Black people received the opportunity to live and even work in the White House. A Black man named Barack Obama was even elected as President of the United States of America. President John F. Kennedy, Jr. (1917-1963) was assassinated because he was a Christian and was using his

Introduction: A Valley Experience

position to advance the lives of others. Kennedy's death was not in vain because we now have the opportunity to live in a world with benefits that allow us to help struggling people. Rev. Dr. Martin Luther King, Jr. (1929-1968) was a Christian warrior. He was on the battlefield marching for equal rights, equal pay, and equal treatment of all people. Dr. King received a dream from God that we'd all be free at last: Blacks and Whites would walk hand in hand and peacefully protest injustice everywhere; Whites and Blacks would eat together, go to school together, worship together, and live together as sisters and brothers. As Amos 5:24 says, "But let justice run down like water, and righteousness like a mighty stream." Dr. King was also assassinated, but his dream still lives on and his death was not in vain. Today, all people are free to worship, shop, live, work, eat, and go to schools and colleges together regardless of race; however, Satan is still causing people to suffer. The laws have changed, but racism, sexism, discrimination, attitudes hostile towards Christianity, terrorism, and God-haters still exist. The evil spirit behind injustice is Satan. Christians have and are being killed, maimed, crucified, murdered, beheaded, and tortured worldwide. Unimaginable persecutions have occurred throughout history against the body of Christ; but despite of all these tragedies, the gospel is still being preached worldwide. Satan does not have the victory. Countless numbers of people have gotten saved and continue to live for God—and if necessary, die for Christ. Apostle Peter told believers in 1 Peter 4:12-16,

> "Beloved, do not think it strange the fiery trial which is to try you, as though some strange thing happened to you; but rejoice to the extent that you partake of

Christ's sufferings, that when His glory is revealed, you may also be glad with exceeding joy. If you are reproached for the name of Christ, blessed are you, for the Spirit of glory and of God rests upon you. On their part He is blasphemed, but on your part He is glorified. But let none of you suffer as a murder, thief, an evil doer, or as a busybody in other people's matters. Yet if anyone suffers as a Christian, let him not be ashamed, but let him glorify God in this matter."

God rewards those who are faithful to Him; so, if you're in the spiritual valley of Christian suffering, endure with faith, love, holiness, and joyfulness.

You may be in one or more valley experiences at the same time. You may feel defeated physically, mentally, socially, sexually, spiritually, and/or emotionally, but remember that even though you are going through, God is the key to your survival. God is awesome and He has given us the keys needed to make it to the other side of these valleys:

1. God First
2. Look Up
3. Don't Walk Away
4. Get Shelter
5. Get The Word
6. Praise Your Way Through
7. Pray
8. Speak Success
9. Learn To Love
10. God First and Last

Chapter 1

KEY 1: GOD FIRST

"But seek first the kingdom of God and His righteousness, and all these things shall be added to you."—Matthew 6:33

When a divorce, sickness, loss of a job, loss of a parent, loss of possessions, or another valley experience occurs in your life, please put God first. God is our creator, maker, friend, and Father. God is everything. When it feels like you are in a valley, you might wonder about just how do you put God first. Putting God first means making God priority above all. You may be sad, sick, lonely, or depressed when you think about your valley, but you can feel glad, healthy, comforted, and happy if you think about the goodness of God. You could have died in the valley; but since you are still alive, be thankful. Satan is the enemy, not God. Satan comes to steal, kill, and destroy, but Jesus came so that we might have life abundantly.

You may be broke, bitter, busted, and disgusted, but this is just a temporary experience. The good thing about the valley experience is that God knows how to exalt you from a low place. In the beginning, God made heaven and earth: hills and mountains; and don't forget, He made the valleys also. God is allowing, not causing, you to go through the valley, and you will survive the valley experience. God has a plan and will turn your bitterness into sweetness; He'll turn your pain into a testimony, your brokenness into wholeness, and your disgust into joy if you make Him priority in your life. If you put God first, He will not leave you in the "valleys" of life.

God is a father figure. Earthly fathers want the best for their children and would climb the highest mountains and search the lowest valleys should their children get lost; and similarly, you were lost in the valley, got knocked down, took a few bumps and bruises. But look up! God is coming for you! God never gives up. He will help you survive. He'll clean you up and bring you out of that valley.

We must put God first in every area of our lives: in our families, finances, futures, faith, health, wealth, marriages, jobs, salvation, physical bodies, medical situations, emotions, social lives, etc.

GOD 1ST IN FAMILY

We put God first in our families by making God #1. God comes before our spouses, children, and relatives. Pleasing God is more important than pleasing people. Joshua said,

> "And if it seems evil to you to serve the Lord, choose for yourselves this day whom you will serve, whether the gods which your fathers served that were on the other side of the River or the gods of the Amorites in whose land you dwell. But as for me and my house,

Chapter 1: Key 1: God First

we will serve the Lord" (Joshua 24:15).

We live in the world, but do not have to bow down to the god of this worldly system. When God is first and foremost in your family, your family will be under continuous blessings. Families should worship together, pray together, work together, and study together. The family was created by God, and the only way families will survive valley experiences is by making God first.

God teaches family members to love, submit, and work together. Working as a team will strengthen the family. Parents must train up their children to follow after God. Little ones can be taught to pray and praise the Lord. Teenagers can be taught to read the Bible, worship God, and abstain from premarital sex, alcohol, and drugs. Children cannot raise themselves. They don't possess the physical, mental, and cognitive ability to function on their own in life; thus, it is very important that God, mothers, and fathers have a role in rearing them. Children need love, discipline, and our encouragement to grow and develop. Parents should not neglect their children's spiritual, physical or emotional needs. Adults can be trained to talk respectfully and lovingly to one another. Husbands and wives should honor God and remain faithful to their families. Children who grow up in a loving and godly family have a greater chance of teaching their children to live holy, moral, and righteous lives. Holiness is not a feeling; it is a way of life.

If a tragedy strikes a family such as a sickness, fire, or a death, the family will be strong enough to survive if God is in the family. It is hard to lose a loved one or go through illnesses with relatives; the only thing that you can do is put them in the Lord's hands. God is a healer, and if the person dies in Christ we know that death is not the end for them. When a family member becomes deceased, remember the love and good times that you shared and believe that you will be reunited with them again eternally.

Extra-marital affairs destroy relationships; it causes couples to become distant from each other, argue, and lie about their locations. Honesty and trust are broken by adultery and the love the couples once shared soon vanishes and their marriages then fall into trouble. What to do when you don't know what to do? The answer is to humble yourself, pray, and seek God's face. Realize that God is the answer to the most difficult questions in life and can give you strength to be faithful. God will give the spouse strength to forgive the sin of infidelity. It is God who is Love and He'll be an example of how to love one another forever. Marriage takes work, and you must be willing to make sacrifices for it to survive. God works in marriages.

God wants couples to stay married, but divorce happens. Divorce is hard on individuals and children. If a divorce happens because the relationship couldn't be restored, parents still need to be peaceable towards one another. Miracle do happen and divorced couples do remarry and become reconciled back to a loving marriage. To avoid divorce, couples should communicate with God and with each other before they consult anyone else. God is the glue that holds families and marriages together, and they survive by making God priority.

GOD 1ST IN FINANCE

We must put God first in our finances. God comes before our needs and wants. Malachi 3:10 states, "Bring all the tithes into the storehouse, That there may be food in My

Chapter 1: Key 1: God First

house, and try Me now in this," says the Lord of host, "If I will not open for you the windows of heaven and pour out for you such a blessing that there will not be room enough to receive it." God only asks for 10% of your income, which means if you have $1,000 give $100, $100 give $10, and $10 give $1. If you are faithful with the small amount, God will increase your income and cause many blessings to overtake you. Also, you can give additional offerings above the tithes. When God is first in our finances, we will be blessed and will have enough for both us and others. God's financial plan consists of the tithe, the offerings, saving, lending, and being a blessing to others in obedience to Christ.

Jesus said, "It is more blessed to give than to receive" (Acts 20:35b). Give freely to the poor, the church, charity, missions, and to others. Giving financial gifts is sharing, and if you give God will give it back to you. Luke 6:38 says, "Give, and it will be given to you; good measure, pressed down, shaken together, and running over will be put into your bosom. For with the same measure that you use, it will be measured back to you." God wants us to live prosperous lives in all areas including finance. If you do not have any money to give, you can give time, talents, gifts of love, possessions, and thanks.

A part of God's financial plan is saving. Proverbs 30:25 states, "The ants are a people not strong, yet they prepare their food in the summer." We see ants gathering up food because they know that winter is coming; they have food stored up ahead of time. If we live long enough, winter will come to us and we will not be able to work like we once did. God wants us to save some of our finances, but He also cautions us not to put our trust in our money. Never say, "I am rich, have become wealthy, and have need of nothing" (Revelation 3:17a). God gives us the knowledge, power, and strength to gain wealth, and we'll always need Him. Your heavenly treasure is more secure than any earthly bank, retirement plan, investment, or savings account. Participate in things that will add to your heavenly account—things such as salvation, faith, love, peace, joy, giving, and sharing.

Also, God wants us to be the lender, not the borrower. Proverbs 19:17 says, "He who has pity on the poor lends to the Lord, and He will pay back what he has given." In the world's system, we borrow and borrow then have to repay interests on that money, and this places us in great debt. But God says, "And you shall remember the Lord your God, for it is He who gives you the power to get wealth, that He may establish His covenant which He swore to your fathers, as it is this day"(Deuteronomy 8:18). Moral people lend to others, but wicked people borrow and do not repay. The wealth of the wicked is going to be transferred to the righteous because God needs people who will seek and support His kingdom. That's why God blesses us.

Choose to obey God in your finances and obey Him in all other areas of your life. You will be blessed even when you go through valley experiences. Thank God for His abundant supplies and new mercies each day.

When God gave the children of Israel the first covenant; He knew that they would not be able to fully keep it because of the sin nature; thus, a new everlasting and greater covenant was created by God, one that allows generations and all people to become heirs to better promises. We see God in Christ's nature and blessings in Christ's obedience. Jesus Christ fulfilled the law. Because we have Jesus' faith we have the right to earthly, spiritual, and heavenly

CHAPTER 1: KEY 1: GOD FIRST

blessings. The old covenant was fear and works based, but the new covenant is love, faith, and grace based. Now, we keep God's commandments because we love Him and not because we will be destroyed if we don't. We love our families, friends, children, church family, neighbors, associates, strangers, and even enemies because we love God with all our hearts. We want our families, friends, children, associates, strangers, neighbors, enemies, and all people to come to Jesus Christ, too. We follow God's law of love not out of fear of being caught, but because as believers His Spirit lives in us. If we sin we do not lose our salvation, but we do not use grace as a free pass to continue in sins. Sinful people break covenants; God does not. Do we continue to get God's blessings, even when disobedient? When we repent, believe in Jesus' complete obedience, we are justified by faith and get blessings we don't lawfully qualify for. God is kind, merciful, generous, gracious, and blesses us because of Jesus' obedience (coming to the earth, going to the cross, dying on the cross for men's sins, and rising from the dead), which was an act of love. The new covenant is blood bought and spiritual. We are blessed when our sins and iniquities are forgiven; it's then that nothing and no one can prevent us from receiving God's blessings. God's new covenant gives us numerous blessings:

- Spiritual Blessings (salvation, eternal life, love, power, Holy Spirit, tongues, miracles, visions, signs, wonders, joy, born again, holiness, anointing, favor, armor of God, grace, mercy, prophecy, righteousness, faith, kingdom of heaven, kingdom of God)
- Physical Blessings (healing, rest, sobriety, good health, strength, mercy, long life, safety, security, nourishment)

- Financial Blessings (overflow, prosperity, money, houses, lands, cars, jobs, businesses, multiple sources of income, cheerful giving, scholarships, debt cancelations, debt free living)
- Mental Blessings (peace, sound mind, clarity, clear thinking, sanity, renewed mind, awareness, good memory, contentment)
- Family/Social Blessings (generational blessings, children, church family, marriage, brothers and sisters, mothers and fathers, love and relationships)
- Emotional Blessings (hope, endurance, relaxation, comfort, Godly sorrow producing repentence, eternal consolation, courage, compassion, happiness, thankfulness, kindness)
- Sexual Blessings (fulfilling sex in marriage, fidelity, self-control, virginity, purity, deliverance from sexual immorality)

The new covenant is superior to the old covenant, for we are blessed because of Jesus' obedience. We have the indwelling of the Holy Spirit and a promise of an imperishable crown and eternal life with Jesus. On earth, we experience promotion and increase on our jobs. We are promised peaceful homes and communities. Prosperity in our health and finances is all because of Jesus. God supernaturally meets our daily needs and gives us fruitful families. We sow and reap a bountiful harvest when we plant seeds into the lives of others. An outpouring of God's favor rest upon us and we have wisdom, proper money management skills, and good and perfect gifts.

GOD 1ST IN OUR FUTURE

Chapter 1: Key 1: God First

We also put God first in our future. As humans, we cannot predict future events, but God can because He created it all. The Bible contains prophetic events- some fulfilled and some to be fulfilled. There are true prophets and prophetess among us, and there are also false lying prophets and prophetess that God did not send. If you spend your time worrying about future events you will not focus on God's goodness today. Worry produces depression, anxiety, stress, mental, and emotional problems. So trust God for your future. God says, "There is hope for your future, says the Lord, that your children shall come back to their own border" (Jeremiah 31:17). You may be going through right now, but still have hope in God. Jeremiah had the right attitude in Lamentations 3:21-24, "This I recall to my mind, therefore I have hope. Through the Lord's mercies we are not consumed; because His compassions fail not. They are new every morning; great is Your Faithfulness, 'The Lord is my portion,' says my soul, 'therefore I hope in Him!'". As we hope in God, even in the difficult and perilous times we do not fear. Our hope, faith, strength, identity, trust, and belief must be in God the Father, Jesus the Christ, and the Holy Spirit.

GOD 1ST IN FAITH

We put God first in our faith. Faith is belief and trust. We live by faith, for "faith is the substance of things hoped for and the evidence of things not seen" (Hebrews 11:1). As believers, we place our faith completely in Jesus Christ who purchased our redemption, salvation, healing, deliverance, justification, fruits of the Spirit, and righteousness by shedding his blood on the cross. Jesus is the Son of God (God in the flesh) and He left heaven and came to this cruel world to live and die. Jesus ministered to people, healed the sick, delivered demon possessed, raised the dead, preached the gospel, and did many other miracles that are recorded in the Holy Bible. He then laid down His life for us and was raised from the dead on the third day (Matthew 28). We place our faith in Jesus for healing and salvation and in all areas of our lives. God is not dead. He is available to heal and save if we have faith. When trials come and valley experiences show up, do not let your faith be destroyed. Peter knew we would face trials as followers of Christ, but he gives us reasons to have faith, 1 Peter 1:6-8:

> "In this you greatly rejoice, though now for a little while, if need be, you have been grieved by various trials, that the genuineness of your faith, being more precious than gold that perishes, though it is tested by fire, may be found to praise, honor, and glory at the revelation of Jesus Christ, whom having not seen you love. Though now you do not see Him, yet believing, you rejoice with joy inexpressible and full of glory, receiving the end of your faith- the salvation of your souls."

Real faith is not giving up in the face of valley experiences. Real faith is going on when all the people who said they love you walk away. Real faith endures to the end. The way out of the valley you are going through is to trust God and always put God first, for He will get you through. Faith is very important to Christians. We live, walk, love, are justified, saved, are healed, and are overcomers by faith. We must put our faith in God and not the things of this world. Faith in Christ is vital to our survival of a valley experience

Chapter 1: Key 1: God First

because without faith we would have no expectation of living above our present situations. We need God. We cannot walk, talk, live, breathe, move, or survive without Him. God is the top priority and to survive God must be first in our marriages, health, families, finances, sex lives, minds, emotions, spirits, souls, futures, and faith.

God 1st in wisdom

God is also first in wisdom. The wisdom of God is unsearchable. No human can create a universe made with animals, plants, man, the clouds, stars, the sun, moon, trees, seas, lands, earth, and nature; and not to overlook all the natural resources God has and the precious metals that belong to Him such as gold, silver, diamonds, gemstones, pearls, sapphires, rubies, and others. God is supreme ruler over heaven and earth and we need to come to Him for Godly counsel. Naked, we came into the world and naked (without earthly possessions) we will leave this world. Instead of seeking stuff, we should seek the kingdom of God and God's wisdom. God's infinite wisdom provided us a way out of our valley experiences through Jesus. Proverbs 9:10 says, "The fear of the Lord is the beginning of wisdom, and the knowledge of the Holy One is understanding." The wisest thing we can do is to believe and accept Jesus Christ as Lord and Savior. 1 Corinthians 1:30 says, "But of Him you are in Christ Jesus, who became for us wisdom from God-and righteousness and sanctification and redemption." Jesus teaches His disciples how to live, have faith, give, pray, work, talk, walk, love, and survive wisely.

God gives people wisdom to preach the gospel, make cars, build houses, write books, advance in technology, communicate with others, get and stay healthy, excel in school, prosper in money, and survive adversity. God is the

source of wisdom and we need to first seek God for wisdom in wealth, health, finances, family, childcare, jobs, marriage, emotions, thinking, mind, schools, communities, society, churches, government, friendships, relationships, partnerships, body, soul, and spirit. There is nothing that God does not know. While we try to invent or figure things out; God already has the knowledge and wisdom for everything. What men think is wisdom is foolishness to God. God's wisdom is eternal, lasting from generations until generations. As we ask God and gain His understanding we need to apply wisdom to any valley experiences we go through.
God 1st in health

Put God first in your health. Satan wants you to be sick, ill, and in pain. God wants us to be healed and have a healthy lifestyle. God does not put sickness and diseases on people to punish them for sins. Satan is the originator of lies, sin, disobedience, and sickness. God's plan for our healing is for us to ask for healing, pray for healing, receive healing, and give thanks for healing. We have authority in the Name of Jesus to command foul spirits, sickness, and diseases to flee. We pray over our bodies and expect to heal because healing is available to God's children. We accept healing by faith. We thank God for healing because we know that healing comes from God. As we pray in faith, God reverses the curse of sickness and disease, and we recover. God has also given humans wisdom to use health professionals, diet, exercise, medicine, natural remedies, vitamins, minerals, nutrients and nutrition to help us get well. Doctors and medicines are good, but realize that God is the Healer and God is the first priority. In an emergency situation, call on God first. God gave us breath, hearts, lungs, kidneys, brains, limbs, all other body parts, and also

CHAPTER 1: KEY 1: GOD FIRST

souls, and spirits.

GOD 1ST IN DECISION-MAKING

Put God first in all your decisions. If faced with a challenge, go to God in prayer and go to the Bible to find out His will. God can speak in an audible voice, in a still small voice, in his Holy word, in angelic visitations, through ministers of the word, through prophets, dreams, visions, through the Holy Spirit, and whatever way He deems appropriate. God will not force you or make you obey His will, but always warn you about the consequences of disobedience. Gentle Jesus gives us wisdom, power, love, a sound mind, and the desire to make good decisions; however, if you make bad or wrong choices do not wallow in despair; get up, repent, and try it again. Follow Christ, go back to work or school, forgive your enemies, love others, raise your children right, stop using drugs and alcohol, live holy, and do what God has put in your heart to do. You will not fail if you put God first.

GOD IS FIRST

God is the most important being in our lives. Although things may be going opposite of what you desire, you must seek God. To survive a valley experience put God in the forefront of your steps. He knows the path you are taking and is always with you guarding your body, family, finances, mind, emotions, soul, spirit, and mind.

10 Ways To Survive A Valley Experience

Chapter 2

KEY 2: LOOK UP

"I will lift up my eyes to the hills—From whence comes my help."—Psalm 121:1

In the valley experience, you may feel that life is not worth living and all hope is lost. You may feel weak or to burden down to even get out of your bed and go to work. You may be homeless and lost all earthly possessions. You may be in a hospital bed, nursing home, or in a correctional facility. Nevertheless, please look up. An upward look may seem impossible in the experience you are going through. Time after time you tried to get out of poverty, but you fell right back. You tried to get out of that toxic relationship, but you went right back. You tried to stop smoking, drinking, having premarital sex and using drugs, but the temptation was too strong. Now you feel that you are losing the battle and why should you look up. You should look up because all of your help is coming from God.

10 Ways To Survive A Valley Experience

REDEEMED FROM DESTRUCTION

In the Bible (1 and 2 Samuel), King David is the best example of a person who looked up in a valley experience. David's life consisted of many highs and lows. He faced giants, moral failures, sickness, enemies, committed crimes, had victories, and repented of wrongdoing. Born into a lineage of noble people, David had the opportunity to become king. But his father, Jesse, made him the keeper of the sheep and David was not considered by man for a kingly position. God looked at his heart and not his outward appearance and circumstances and David was anointed as king years before he got the throne. 1 Samuel 16:7 says, "But the Lord said to Samuel, 'Do not look at his appearance or at his physical stature because I have refused him. For the Lord does not see as a man sees; for man looks at the outward appearance, but the Lord looks at the heart.'" David fought Goliath, gained popularity, served as psalmist to King Saul, and then he became king himself. King Saul wanted to kill David, his sons wanted him dead, he committed adultery, and he murdered innocent people. I am sure that David was so defeated and he needed God's help. He had let himself down, his nation down, his friends down, and his family down. David's love affair with sin was finally over. David knew how to get out the valley – look up. David needed a new heart so old sins would not corrupt him and cause God pain. In Psalm 51:7-11, David writes:

> "Purge me with hyssop and I shall be clean. Wash me and I shall be whiter than snow. Make me hear joy and gladness. That the bones you have broken may rejoice. Hid your face from my sins and blot out all my iniquities. Create in me a clean heart and

Chapter 2: Key 2: Look Up

renew a steadfast spirit within me. Do not cast me away from your presence and do not take your Holy Spirit from me."

David is powerful because he always had an upward look. Although the valley is low, you look up. God will look down where you are and pick you up and place you where you belong–on a rock. I know it is not easy to look up in a valley experience, but if you look up you will survive. Looking up will give you a new heart and perspective on life. Yes, you are in the valley. Yes, you did sin. Yes, you did wrong to yourself and others. Yes, God still sees you where you are and He will forgive you and give you your joy back. It is not as bad as it seems because the price has already been paid for salvation. God sent His Son (Jesus) to rescue us from a valley of sin and death. Look up to Jesus.

If we are going to look up we need to see Jesus. Hebrews 12:2 states, "looking unto Jesus, the author and finisher of our faith, who for the joy that was set before Him endured the cross, despising the shame, and has sat down at the right hand of the throne of God." We look up to God for salvation. Psalm 5:3 says, "My voice You shall hear in the morning, O Lord; In the morning I will direct it to You, and I will look up." Every day you rise, talk to God in prayer, give thanksgiving, and look unto Him for strength to go through the daily journey. Isaiah 45:22 states, "Look to me, and be saved, all you ends of the earth. For I am God and there is no other." We need to get in a position that God will be the focus of our existence.

As we look onto God, we are lifted up. We lift up our heads, eyes, hands, soul, and voice to the Almighty.

LIFTED HEADS

Our head is at the top of our body and we have a brain that is the center of our thought and mind processes. Jesus Christ is our spiritual head and we lift our heads to Him for wisdom, sound mind, and peace. Psalm 24:7-8 states, "Lift up your heads, O you gates! And be ye lifted up, you everlasting doors! And the King of glory shall come in. Who is this King of glory? The Lord strong and mighty, the Lord mighty in battle." Gates and doors are synonymous with coming in or access. To open the door for God to come in we must have a mind stayed on Christ. When God comes in, He will fight our battles. Therefore, if your enemies and Satan attack your mental state, God will come in to bring you peace, safety, and security in the midst of valley experiences. Psalm 27:6 states, "And now my head shall be lifted up above my enemies all around me; Therefore I will offer sacrifices of joy in His tabernacle; I will sing, yes I will sing praises to the Lord." When God has our head/mind covered like David says in Psalm 4:8: "I will both lie down in peace, and sleep; for you alone, O Lord make me dwell in safety." Lift up your head and look up. God is the lifter of bowed down heads and He redeems our lives.

LIFTED EYES

The eyes are the part of our body concerning what we see in the natural and spiritual. Sometimes people can experience eye problems and lose their vision, physically as well as spiritual. As we lift up our eyes to Jesus, He heals any difficulties we have.

BLINDNESS

Blindness is the physical lack of sight. People can be born

Chapter 2: Key 2: Look Up

blind or have a disease or accident that causes them to lose their sight. Spiritual blindness is a condition of being ignorant of God's ways. Spiritually blind people have no dreams and no vision for themselves or others. Jesus says in Luke 6:39, "Can the blind lead the blind? Will they not both fall into the ditch?"

Satan has blinded many people eyes with unbelief, lust, and self-righteousness. They are falling into a pit of hell and are unaware of the dangerous paths they take. Thankfully, Jesus is the cure for both physical and spiritual blindness. Psalm 146:8 says, "The Lord opens the eyes of the blind; The Lord raises those who are bowed down; The Lord loves the righteous." When we come to Jesus and look up, we get His sight. We can come out of the valley and see clearly to help someone else.

NEARSIGHTEDNESS

Nearsightedness means that your eyes have difficulty focusing on distant objects. You see well up close, but cannot see correctly at a far distance. Spiritual nearsightedness can occur in a valley experience. As you move further away from God, you lose your focus. God has been good to you in your past and present, but you are unsure about the future. You endure for a while, but give up when you do not see your help. God has not moved- you have lost focus. Mercifully, God cures physical and spiritual nearsightedness. Psalm 121:2 says, "My help comes from the Lord, who made heaven and earth." Look up and receive the sight to trust God at all times. Your future is secure if you have made Jesus Christ Lord and Savior. After Jesus' resurrection in John 20:29, "Jesus said to him, Thomas, because you have seen Me, you have believed. Blessed are those who have not seen and yet have believed." Faith in a BIG God cures spiritual nearsightedness.

FARSIGHTEDNESS

Farsightedness means that your eyes have difficulty focusing on near objects. You see objects better far away but cannot see them up close. Spiritual farsightedness occurs when we trust God for our future, but do not trust Him for our present situation. For example, you say incorrect things like: "I know God will heal, provide, deliver, but I just can't see it happening right now," "I can't see God in this valley," etc. God is always near, but you miss Him in the everydayness of life. Yes, God heals sickness, provides money, food, clothing, and shelter, delivers the oppressed, and sets captives free. God cures physical and spiritual farsightedness if we lift up our eyes to Him. Psalm 123:1-2 says, "Unto you I lift up my eyes, O You who dwell in the heavens. Behold, as the eyes of servants look to the hand of their masters, as the eyes of a maid to the hand of her mistress, so our eyes look the Lord our God until He has mercy on us." God presently has mercy on us, heals us right now, and has already made a way for us. Look up and don't doubt God. We must focus on God's vision for our lives. Faith is not about what you can see, but it is about Who is your God. See yourself like God sees you. God sees you as healed, delivered, wealthy, blessed, saved, valuable, victorious, a survivor.

ASTIGMATISM

Astigmatism is a defect in the eyes preventing proper focusing. Astigmatism sufferers may squint and have distorted vision and have trouble seeing up close and at a distance. Spiritual Astigmatism occurs when you take your focus off

Chapter 2: Key 2: Look Up

Jesus and put it on your circumstances. You have a distorted and incorrect view of God, yourself, and others. You are like the parable of the sower sowing seeds on the rock in Luke 8:13, " But the ones on the rock are those who, when they hear, receive the word with joy, and these have not root, who believe for a while and in the time of temptation fall away." You collapse in the valley experiences because you have taken your eyes off Jesus. God cures physical and spiritual astigmatism. Hebrews 4:15-16 says, "Seeing then that we have a great High Priest who has passed through the heavens, Jesus the Son of God, let us hold fast our confession. For we do not have a High Priest who cannot sympathize with our weakness, but was in all points tempted as we are, yet without sin." Look up to Jesus. Being tempted is not sin, temptation becomes sin when we are led away and act on sinful desires.

CATARACTS AND GLAUCOMA

Cataracts and glaucoma are diseases of the eyes. Cataract is a clouding of the lens of the eyes and blurry vision occurs. Glaucoma is a disease that causes a buildup of fluid in the eye and an increase of the pressure in the eyes. Left untreated cataracts and glaucoma can lead to blindness. Spiritual cataracts and glaucoma are when things come and obscure our focus of Jesus. The pressures of life build up and you cannot focus on Jesus' word in your heart. You are like seed sown and thorns come in to choke it found in Luke 8:14: "Now the ones that fell among thorns, are those who, when they have heard, go out and are choked with cares, riches, and pleasures of life, and bring no fruit to maturity." You become blinded by greed, lust, partying, earthly pleasures, and can fall into sin and idolatry; however, Jesus heals physical and spiritual cataracts and glaucoma. 1 John 2:15-16 says, "Do not love the world or the things in the world. If anyone loves the world, the love of the Father is not in Him. For all that is in the world –the lust of the flesh, the lust of the eyes, and the pride of life- is not of the Father, but is of the world." David says in Psalm 25:15, "My eyes are ever toward the Lord, for He shall pluck my feet out of the net." Look up to Jesus for forgiveness and restoration of your sight. Psalm 119:18 states, "Open my eyes, that I may see wondrous things from Your law." Look up.

OPTICAL ILLUSIONS

Satan tries to bring you an optical illusion of false prosperity. You may see celebrities who live ungodly or immoral lives, but still accumulate material comfort, designer clothes, diamonds, fleets of cars, money in multiple banks, and mansions. We see outward success, but inwardly these celebrities can be depressed, suicidal, and addicted to fame, alcohol, porn, sex, gambling, and/ or drugs. Unfortunately, when Satan is finished with them he throws them away like a dirty rag, devours their lives completely, and/ or bankrupts their marriages, bodies, and minds. But there is a God in heaven, who gives true prosperity. True prosperity is found in God who keeps your mind in perfect peace when you look to Jesus. True prosperity is hearing the word of God, understanding the word, believing in the word, trusting in God, and living by faith. The things that are seen in the world are earthly/carnal and the things seen in the spirit are heavenly/eternal.

Satan wants to steal, kill, and destroy the word of God, the witness of Jesus, and worship of God. Satan knows his time is coming to an end and does not want peo-

Chapter 2: Key 2: Look Up

ple souls' to be saved. Jesus says in Matthew 24:14, "And this gospel of the kingdom will be preached in all the world as a witness to all the nations, and then the end will come." Satan wishes for world leaders, athletes, celebrities, preachers, ministers, singers, and others promote a false counterfeit religion. "And the Lord said, 'Simon, Simon! Indeed, Satan has asked for you, that he may sift you as wheat. 'But I have prayed for you, that your faith should not fail; and when you have returned to Me, strengthen you brethren'" (Luke 2:31-32). Faith will not fail if it is in the right One –Jesus. In the midst of a valley experience, do not look to the world system, have faith in Christ. Stand on the word of God, witness about Jesus, and worship God.

Be not deceived; true kingdom riches is only found by faith in Jesus Christ. The love of money is deception. Jesus asked in Matthew 16:26, "For what profit is it to a man if he gains the whole world, and loses his own soul? Or what will a man give in exchange for his soul?" There are some things that money just can't buy. Money can buy a house, but can't buy a peaceful home. Money can buy stiletto heels or shoes, but cannot buy mobility. Money can buy a pacemaker, but cannot buy a new and clean heart. Money can buy a bed, but cannot buy restful sleep. Money can buy sex, but cannot buy love. Money can buy diamond rings, but cannot buy commitment. Money can buy electricity, but cannot buy Holy Ghost power. Money can buy prescription drugs, but can't buy health and healing. Money can buy an alarm system, but can't buy protection. Money can buy food, but cannot buy an appetite. Money can't buy salvation – salvation is free. Salvation is free to all who believe in the Lord Jesus Christ.

LIFTED HANDS

The hands are also part of the body that we lift up to God. We raise our hands to God because Jesus is the answer. We lift our hands as surrender, worship, and sacrifice. Hands sometimes get dirty from sinful works of the flesh and devil. As we lift our hands to God, we tell the flesh "no", tell the devil "you are no longer my father", and are saying to God "clean me up". We surrender all to Jesus, because He destroyed the works of the devil and has become our Master. Psalms 143:6 says, "I spread out my hands to You; My soul longs for You like a thirsty land." Going through a valley experience, we surrender everything to God (spirit, soul, and body). Lord, here are our hands; we give them to you. Use our hands for your service. Use our hands to help others, give to the poor and the church, lay on the sick, feed the hungry, work in Your kingdom, serve our communities, touch lives, and hold hands and pray for and with others.

We lift our hands in worship and prayer. Paul said to Timothy, "I desire therefore that the men pray everywhere, lifting up holy hands, without wrath and doubting"(I Timothy 2:8). David says in Psalm 28:2, "Hear the voice of my supplications when I cry to You, when I lift up my hands toward Your holy sanctuary." As we come into worship, we lift our hands toward God knowing that He is holy, worthy, and righteous. We adore Him and know He is everything.

We also lift up our hands as a sacrifice. Psalm 141:2 says, "Let my prayer be set before You as incense, The lifting up of my hands as the evening sacrifice." God sacrificed for us and we have no problems lifting up our hands to Him. Jesus' hands and feet were nailed to a cross for us. Psalm 134:2 says, Lift up your hands in the sanctuary, and bless the Lord. Give God the Glory and forget about yourself.

Chapter 2: Key 2: Look Up

LIFTED SOUL

The soul is the part of our being that contains our mind, will, and emotions. We lift up our soul to God for His ways, His statues, gladness, and His guidance. David writes in Psalm 25:1-5 as he goes after God's righteous path:

> "To You O Lord, I lift up my soul. O my God, I trust in You; let me not be ashamed; let not my enemies triumph over me. Indeed, let no one who waits on You be ashamed; let those be ashamed who deal treacherously without cause. Show me your ways, O Lord; Teach me your paths, Lead me in Your truth and teach me, For You are the God of my salvation; On You I wait all day."

As we lift our souls to God, He teaches us how to live truthful, merciful, and integral lives.

Also, we find joy when we lift our souls to God. Sons of Korah writes in Psalm 42:1-2: "As the deer pants for the water brooks, so pants my soul for You, O God. My soul thirsts for God, for the living God, when shall I come and appear before God?" Going through the valley experiences, we experience a variety of emotions and we may cry, scream, sob, get angry, and upset. The answer to our joy being restored in the valley is Jesus. David writes in Psalm 86:4-5, "Rejoice the soul of your servant, for to You, O Lord, I lift up my soul. For You Lord, are good and ready to forgive, and abundant in mercy to all those who call upon You." We all experience stress in our lives and want to give up on assignments, callings, and happiness. I recommend that when we are in a low mental or emotional place: start to read the Bible, listen to sermons, listen to calming gospel music, pray, and meditate on God's word. Things do not always go the way that we plan but remember God is still in control. Look Up.

As we lift our souls to God, we also receive His guidance. Guidance means to direct or lead the way for someone. God has to guide us away from things that are harmful to us and guide us toward the things that are helpful. David writes in Psalm 143:8, "Cause me to hear Your lovingkindness in the morning, for in You do I trust; cause me to know the way in which I should walk, for I lift up my soul to You." Lord God leads us into good plans, thoughts, jobs, relationships, thinking, and living. Isaiah writes; "The Lord will guide you continually, and satisfy your soul in drought, and strengthen your bones; you shall be like a watered garden, and like a spring of water, whose waters do not fail" (58:11). God has given us the Bible as our road map, Jesus Christ as our way, and the Holy Spirit as our guide. We will reach our destination and come out of the valley experiences as we lift our souls to God.

LIFTED VOICE

The voice is the sound produced by our mouth when speaking to God, others, or self. Everyone has a distinct and unique voice-some soft, others loud. God knows each of His children's voice and hears us we speak. We lift up our voices unto God by singing, praying, speaking, crying out, shouting, and making joyful noises of praise. God gave us our voices and said, "Let everything that has breath praise the Lord. Praise the Lord" (Psalm 150:6). We can sing with or without music and make melodies in our hearts. Ephesians 5:18-19 says, "And do not be filled with wine, in which

Chapter 2: Key 2: Look Up

is dissipation, but be filled with the Spirit, Speaking to one another in psalms and hymns, and spiritual songs, singing and making melody in your heart to the Lord." Psalm 66:1-4 says, "Make a joyful shout to God, all the earth! Sing out the honor of His name; make His praise glorious. Say to God, How awesome are Your works! Through the greatness of your power Your enemies shall submit themselves to You. All the earth shall worship You and sing praises to You; they shall sing praises to Your name." No matter what valley you are going through, praise God for His awesome power. Look up and give God praise. Sing unto the Lord about His mercy and justice. Praise is a weapon against the enemy of fear and depression. Praise God because of His excellent supremacy, mighty acts, and saving grace.

As you go through the valley experience, remember to look up. God will lead you and guide you out. You will survive the trials and storms of life if you stay focused on Jesus and surrender all to Him. We do not have to walk around with our heads hang down low, all we need to do is look to Jesus Christ and He will completely save us.

10 Ways To Survive A Valley Experience

Chapter 3

KEY 3: DON'T WALK AWAY

"...Indeed the Lord gave Job twice as much as he had before."—Job 42:10b

A VALLEY IS A LOW PLACE BETWEEN TWO HIGH OR elevated areas; therefore, when you leave a valley, you must go higher physically, socially, financially, mentally, emotionally, sexually, and spiritually. Stay with God because He will take you to higher ground where you need to be and belong.

DOUBLE

In the book of Job, we see a man who experienced a true low place (valley). Job was a wealthy businessman, a good father and husband, and a servant of God. Satan tested Job's faith in God with losses and a sickness in his body. Job lost his possessions, wealth, children; his health failed and his friends became few, but Job never lost his faith. When Job was sick—his body covered with boils—his wife told him to curse God and die, but Job did not listen to her. He told her that she was speaking foolishly. Job had determined within himself that he would not walk away from God - we need that determination also. In times of desperation and struggle, the easiest thing to do is turn away from God. Satan thought that if Job lost God's hedge of protection, he would decide to leave God and abandon his integrity; nevertheless, Job remained faithful and did not walk away from God in the midst of his valley experience. What if Job would have cursed God? The book of Job would not be a survival manual for us. You see, Job received double that which he lost in the end. God restored Job physically, financially, mentally, emotionally, and spiritually. Because Job stayed close to God during his adversity, he got healed and received twice as much as before. Job 42:12 says, "Now the Lord blessed the latter days of Job more than his beginning; for he had fourteen thousand sheep, six thousand camels, one thousand yokes of oxen, and one thousand female donkeys." God is no respecter of persons. If you stay with God in the valley, you too will come out with double. Job stayed close to the only true source of purpose, healing, wisdom, riches and favor. "'God,' Job says, 'I know that You can do everything, And that no purpose of Yours can be withheld from You'" (Job 42:2). God created the world, our surroundings, every spirit/soul, and our bodies, and He can fix that which is broken if we repent and seek Him with our hearts; if we do so, we'll then regain everything that we lost.

DO NOT WALK AWAY

Walking towards God beats walking away from God. God provides blessings and eternal life, but Satan brings curses and death. The further you move away from God, the worse your state will be physically, mentally, socially, emo-

Chapter 3: Key 3: Don't Walk Away

tionally, spiritually, financially, and sexually. Proverbs 24:16 says, "For a righteous man may fall seven times and rise again, But the wicked shall fall by calamity." If you happen to fall, get back up and start walking towards God. Dont' run from God, especially if you're in a valley.

Maybe you believe that the things you did, thought, and said were too evil for God to forgive. Maybe you have been sinning for a long time and have walked away from the church, your family, and God; but God is a forgiving God, and He is able to cleanse you from all unrighteousness. God knows all about what you are going through. Psalm 99:8 says, "You answered them, O Lord our God; You were to them God who forgives though You took vengeance on their deeds." God hates the sin but loves the sinner. Don't walk away. God has provided forgiveness for ALL of our sins and has given us grace through Jesus Christ.

Walking towards God as opposed to walking away from God carries many benefits—

Walking to God	**Walking away from God**
Light	Darkness
Help	Helplessness
Hope	Hopelessness
Life	Death
Multiplication	Subtraction
Joy	Sadness
Peace	Hate
Health	Sickness
Love	Fear
Strength	Weakness

Forgiveness	Un-forgiveness
Salvation	Separation
Connection	Disconnection
Favor	Curse
Steadfastness	Unstable
Adoption	Abandonment
Rescue	Captivity
Freedom	Fugitive
Eternal life	Hell
Wisdom	Foolishness
Righteousness	Ungodly
Goodness	Evil

Accepting and following God is the best choice that anyone could ever make. Jesus said in John 8:12, "I am the light of the world. He who follows Me shall not walk in darkness, but have the light of life." Satan has blinded some with the lust of the flesh, the pride of life, false prosperity, selfish desires, and unbelief. Repent and turn away from these things before you find yourself burning in the lake of fire. Run to God. If people continue to walk in darkness, they will stumble and miss the blessings of God.

STEADFASTNESS VS. UNSTABLE

1 Corinthians 15:58 says, "Therefore my beloved brethren, be steadfast, immovable, always abounding in the work of the Lord, knowing that your labor is not in vain the Lord." Our loyalty should be to Jesus Christ because He made a way for us to survive our valley experiences. We must not

CHAPTER 3: KEY 3: DON'T WALK AWAY

waiver when dark clouds come and strong winds began to blow. James 1:8 says this about those who doubt God: "He is a double-minded man, unstable in all his ways." We must not flip-flop when confronted with the wicked things of the world. We must be stable in Jesus Christ. Jesus gives us physical, mental, financial, family/social, emotional, and sexual stability. We have power through Jesus to withstand the schemes of the devil. Jesus says in Mark 16:17-18, "And these signs will follow those who believe: In My name they will cast out demons; they will speak with new tongues; they will take up serpents; and if they drink anything deadly, it will by no means hurt them; they will lay hands on the sick, and they will recover." Stand on the word of God and know that you are a survivor.

CONNECTED VS. DISCONNECTED

Jesus said, "If anyone does not abide in Me, he is cast out as a branch and it withered; and they gather them and throw them into the fire, and they are burned" (John 15:6). Jesus said He is the vine and we, being the branches, must stay connected to Him in order to survive in this world. Sometimes God will prune us and take away dead things and things that weigh us down. We think God is punishing us when He takes away toxic relationships, fake friends, selfish ambitions, and bad habits, but God is really saving our lives. To boost our spiritual growth, God takes away the things that take our time and attention away from Him. We get overloaded with to-do lists, pursuing goals, and unnecessary desires. Our time of spiritual development would truly be maximized if God was first on our list, heaven was our goal, and our desire was to please God. As we stay connected to Jesus, we bear the fruit of peaceful thoughts, loving relationships, good practices, greater progress, and powerful principles. Jesus is our power source, and if we connect to Him, we will be able to overcome every valley experience. Abide in Christ and His plan.

ADOPTION VS. ABANDONMENT

"Adoption" means "to take and raise a child as your own flesh and blood." On the other hand, "abandonment" means "to forsake entirely, to give up, or leave." We have been adopted into God's family and should never abandon God for the world, flesh, or devil. Romans 8:15 states, " For you did not receive the spirit of bondage again to fear, but you receive the Spirit of adoption, by whom we cry out, Abba, Father." God is a loving, kind, and gracious Daddy. "For you are all sons of God through faith in Jesus Christ" (Galatians 3:26). We are a part of God's family and should, therefore, have a sense of belonging, community, inheritance, and love. Satan is a liar, and in his family, there is murder, fighting, hatred, homosexuality, incest, pride, lust, fornication, adultery, deception, lying, molestation, drunkenness, greed, uncleanness, carnality, jealousy, evil speaking, and other evils. God is the best Father. He will never abuse, neglect, and abandon His children. We have a Godly heritage and should teach our children how to uplift the family of God. God is the truth, and in His family there we find love, peace, joy, long-suffering, kindness, self-control, faith, gentleness, meekness, temperance, purity, morals, grace, mercy, and other blessings. Everyone has to make his or her decision to become a part of God's family by faith through Jesus Christ.

RESCUE VS. CAPTIVITY

CHAPTER 3: KEY 3: DON'T WALK AWAY

All of us were at one point in our lives, walking in the way of sin, but Jesus provided for us all a way of escape. Jesus can deliver us from ungodliness. Without Jesus, we're in danger of hell's fire. Jesus came to give us life. Past sins held us captive, but Jesus took the keys from death and hell so that we may be free. "Captivity" is "the act of being an inmate, prisoner, hostage, or slave to something." It's because of Jesus that we are no longer bound by sin, unbelief, drugs, alcohol, sex, perversions, etc. We can walk away from sin and iniquity and into the loving arms of a Righteous Savior. Jesus said, "Behold, I stand at the door and knock. If anyone hears My voice and opens the door, I will come into him and dine with him and he with Me" (Revelation 3:20). Jesus rescues us when we call on Him. He is our way of escape from the bondage of the world and hell. 1 Corinthians 10:13 says, "No temptation has overtaken you except is common to man, but God is faithful, who will not allow you to be tempted beyond what you are able, but with the temptation will also make the way of escape, that you may be able to bear it." Sometimes, you will be tempted to sin against God, yourself, and others, but you must make the decision to resist temptation. Endure the valley experience. Don't walk away from God – He has the escape route.

FREEDOM VS. FUGITIVE

Jesus says, "Therefore is the son makes you free, you shall be free indeed" (John 8:36). To be free means experiencing liberty and no longer being under the control or power of another. Being a fugitive means to be on the run from something or someone and always look over your shoulder for your captors. God wants us to be completely free from sin. As a fugitive, you are not free; and if you were once free but have since turned your back on God and gone back to the world, then the devil, once he catches you, will certainly enslave you again or kill you. As a child of God, you have a new Master, God, and your old master, Satan, can no longer control you. You cannot free yourself from the bondage of sin and the devil's grip – you need a Savior. Romans 8:2 says, "For the law of the Spirit of life in Christ Jesus has made me free from the law of sin and death." Again, don't walk away or run away from God. We experience true freedom in Christ Jesus. In Christ Jesus, we are free to live victoriously against the world, the flesh, and the devil. Trials may arise and tests may come, but if we are free in Jesus we will survive these trials and tests.

SALVATION VS. SEPARATION

As you are going through your valley experience(s), know that God is with you and you are still saved by grace. Salvation means to be redeemed from sin. Jesus Christ's life, death, burial, and resurrection has provided unto us salvation. Apostle Paul told the Romans, "For I am not ashamed of the gospel of Christ, for it is the power of God to salvation for everyone who believes, for the Jew first and also for the Greek" (Romans 1:16). God does not discriminate against anyone when it comes to being saved. Everyone can be saved: Black or White, rich or poor, male or female. "If we confess our sins, He is faithful and just to forgive us our sins and to cleanse us from all unrighteousness "(1 John 1:9). Salvation allows us to commune, fellowship, and have a relationship with God through faith in Jesus Christ. You will "die in your sins" if you do not believe unto salvation through Jesus (John 8:24). Don't walk away from Jesus. God has provided us salvation through Jesus, and

Chapter 3: Key 3: Don't Walk Away

we do not have to be eternally separated from the Heavenly Father. God will free you from your sins and makes you righteous. As we walk with Jesus, goodness and mercy will accompany us every day.

MULTIPLICATION VS. SUBTRACTION

God does not do math like we do. God is a multiplier - Satan always subtracts. Satan subtracts from us family, peace, finance, health, fidelity, joy, etc. God adds to us life more abundantly. Satan takes good things away. When it feels like you're lost in a valley, do not abandon God. God will multiply His blessings in your life and supply the things you need tremendously. The things we count as losses, God counts them as credit on our behalves. God will restore unto you land, houses, jobs, money, life, love, peace, joy, happiness, health, wealth, justice, blessings, strength, hope, faith, dreams, and visions. God provides us with much more than we can ask or think. Multiplication is God's ultimate plan for our lives.

WHAT TO WALK AWAY FROM

One of the things we need to walk away from is sexual sin. In America, with the passing of same-sex marriage laws, we are heading down a dangerous path of destruction. I am positive homosexuality, fornication, idolatry, murder, adultery, cheating, and lying are sins. As we change our laws to accommodate sin, we are telling God that His laws don't matter. What an indictment against us if we say "In God we trust" on our money but do not trust Him in our bedrooms, government, boardrooms, courtrooms, schools, and even churches. A sin is a sin, and it doesn't matter what particular sin it is and whether or not we've legalized it. We must not take part in the world's way of thinking, less we end up joining forces with those who stand against God.

You might be in a homosexual or immoral sexual relationship and want to get delivered. God is the answer. He will deliver you. Run to Him.

STEPS FOR SEXUAL FREEDOM IN CHRIST JESUS

Admit Sin. Admit that homosexuality and all other sexually immoral and perverse behaviors are sins. God made our sexual parts for procreation and pleasure within the confines of a marriage between one man and one woman only. It is wicked to be involved sexually with those whom God has not joined you with in Holy matrimony. Repent and turn away from sexual sins.

Accept Christ. Accept that Jesus has already died and rose again so that you might be free. Accept that you are not free to continue in a homosexual, immoral and perverse lifestyle. Jesus Christ made you righteous and designed for you to live a sexually moral life. Jesus shed His blood to pay for all of our sins. Jesus came to save the lost, now and forever. Romans 5:21 says, "So that as sin reigned in death, even so grace might reign through righteousness to eternal life through Jesus Christ our Lord." We have died to sexual sin so that we can live for God.

Abort and Abstain from Homosexuality/Immorality/Perversion. Abort unnatural affections and attractions. Put to death sexual feelings and fantasies with people that are of the same sex. Singles, do not lust after someone of the opposite sex if you're not married to him or her. The old nature was crucified with Christ, and you are under no obligation to obey the lusts of the flesh. When Satan brings up sexually perverse and immoral thoughts in your mind, kill them with the word of God. Colossians 3:5-7 says, "Therefore put to death your members which are on the earth: fornication, uncleanness, passion, evil desire, and covetousness, which is idolatry. Because of these things the wrath of God is coming upon the sons of disobedience, in which you yourselves once walked when you lived in them." Abstain from all sexual immorality. Resist the urge to commit fornication and adultery.

Ask God. James 4:3 says, "You ask and do not receive, because you ask amiss, that you may spend it on your pleasures." The desire for sexual pleasure is not wrong, but you become sinful when you go outside of God's parameters to gain sexual fulfillment. Homosexuality, bisexuality, fornication, adultery, child molestation, rape, abuse, pornography, sexual promiscuity, masturbation, etc. are unclean to God. Ask God to send you the husband or wife that He has for you so that you can enjoy a blessed marriage and a healthy sex life. If you are already in a heterosexual marriage, ask God to enhance the intimacy between both of you and help you to remain faithful to one another. God knows the right partners for us and will guide us into godly relationships and loving and prosperous marriages. Pray to God and He will send you who you need as a life partner.

Attend Worship Service. Christians need to go to church and worship God. At church, we are surrounded by other people who share our beliefs. We praise, dance, rejoice, pray, worship, give, sing, listen to scriptures and read them aloud, and hear pastors preach the Gospel. As we feed our spiritual beings, we deprive our flesh. Worship equips God's saints with the courage, knowledge, principles, power, armor, and Word to crush the enemy. As we worship God, God freely gives us whatever we need. God cannot be manipulated. We must worship God in spirit and in truth. Worship God for who He is and also for the victory we have in Jesus. Hebrews 10:25 says, "not forsaking the assembling of ourselves together as is the manner of some, but exhorting one another, and so much the more as you see the Day approaching." We form relationships with people who will encourage us to love God, live holy lives, and pray for others.

UN-FORGIVENESS: THE SILENT KILLER

Also, we need to walk away from unforgiveness. People will talk about you, gossip on you; irritate, agitate and lie to you and on you; abuse and neglect you, misuse you, treat you poorly, mock, divorce, assault and abandon you, and break promises made to you. These actions are not holy. They don't leave you feeling good either. Still, we must forgive. Do not get bitter; instead, let go and get better. God forgave us for all of the sins we have committed against Him, so we must forgive others for their trespasses also. We cannot control the actions of others, but we can control our own actions and reactions. It's important for us to forgive others because we have been forgiven by God. Living in un-forgiveness hurts you more than those you choose not to forgive - they've moved on with their lives and have probably forgotten the whole incident. But because you are stuck in the past and keep reliving the hurt over and over, you can't move on and develop healthy new relationships.

CHAPTER 3: KEY 3: DON'T WALK AWAY

You are trapped in past relationships. Un-forgiveness robs you of love, peace, joy, life, happiness, and your prayer life. Jesus said, "And whenever you stand praying, if you have anything against anyone, forgive him, that your Father in heaven may also forgive you your trespasses. But if you do not forgive, neither will your Father in heaven forgive your trespasses" (Mark 11:25-26). No one has done something so terrible that you can't forgive them. While Jesus was being crucified on the cross, He said, "Father, forgive them for they know not what they do" (Luke 23:34). If God forgives repentant murderers, robbers, homosexuals, rapists, liars, sinners, adulterers, fornicators, persecutors, disobedient children, drunkards, swearers (those who use profane language), abusers, etc., and so can you. God knows everything you've suffered through, but He also knows that un-forgiveness is hurting you more than you know. God said walk away from un-forgiveness and forgive those who have hurt you physically, mentally, emotionally, sexually, financially, socially, spiritually, etc. Forgive one another and walk in love. Get free from unforgiveness. If you cannot forgive yourself and others, you are imprisoned in a mental prison cell. Jesus had come to set you free so that you may live a blessed life. God did not walk away from you, so do not walk away from Him.

We must forgive if we want to make it into the kingdom of God and also survive our valley experiences. When we choose to let go of unforgiveness in our hearts, God will give us the strength to forgive and overcome the painful situations in our lives.

10 Ways To Survive A Valley Experience

CHAPTER 4
KEY 4: GET SHELTER

"He who dwells in the secret place of the Most High shall abide under the shadow of the Almighty. I will say of the Lord, 'He is my refuge and my fortress; My God in Him I will trust."—Psalm 91:1-2

A SHELTER IS SYNONYMOUS WITH PROTECTION OR refuge from danger or distress. In a valley experience, what greater shelter is there to get under than in the secret place of the Most High God. Going through the valleys of life, God is with you and shelters you from the storm. God's secret place is His tabernacle, His presence, His shelter, and His shadow. When the storm of life is brewing and the devil is causing havoc in your mind, family, healthy, job, and life get protection from God. When we as children run to Father God, believe that we can go to Him for help. God is a father and we can cry Abba Father save me and shelter me from this distressing situation and protect me from the enemies all around me.

THE PRODIGAL SON

The prodigal son in Luke 15 is a great example of a son running to his father for shelter. In the narrative summary, a young man asks for his inheritance, leaves his father, wastes his possessions, repents, and then returns back home. I suppose that the son wanted to live a life independent of his father. Although the father was good to the son, the son was tired of being under his authority. He asked for "his portion of goods" (Luke 15:12) and "left for a far country and wasted his possessions with prodigal living" (13). The son thought he was living the good life- fancy clothes, fine dining, cars, shoes, friends, harlots, houses, etc; however, his good time came to a stop and the son found himself in a valley experience. Luke 15:14 says, "But when he had spent all there arose a severe famine in that land and he began to be in want." The son had wasted his money and he was starving and about to die. Then the son had a repentant spirit and wanted to go back to the shelter of his father. "He said, I will arise and go to my father, and will say to him, 'Father I have sinned against heaven and before you, and am no longer worthy to be called your son, make me like one of your hired servants'" (Luke 15:18-19). The prodigal son returned home and the father welcomed him with open arms full of love and compassion and celebrated that his lost son was found.

EVERYTHING IS BETTER WITH GOD

Many times we like the prodigal son have left the protection of our Heavenly Father and gone into a far country. We wanted to live life by ourselves and make our own decisions which often lead to mistakes; however, the consequences of our decisions will have us in valley experiences.

Chapter 4: Key 4: Get Shelter

Fortunately, the way out of the valley is to run back to God for His shelter. Out in the world alone without a Savior we are defenseless against the attacks of the devil. With God we are protected. With God we are saved. With God we are rejoicing. Everything is better with God sheltering us. God is a good Father and brings us back into right relationship with Him if we repent. Repent means to be sorry for the wrongdoing and turn and do what is right. God will bring you out the valley in due time, and will even shelter you while you are still in the low place.

God is a holy God and He doesn't want his children living unholy lives. God wants His children to live a life overflowing in His presence. God's presence gives us abundant joy, love, peace, and happiness. We cannot see God with the naked eye, but we feel His love and see His goodness in creation. God welcomes His children home with pure love and great celebration.

GETTING SHELTER

Getting shelter in God means to come out of the world system, surrender your will to His, and hold on to your faith in Jesus. The prodigal son had to leave the far country behind and come to his father. The world may seem to offer joy and peace, but it's only brief and a misconception. Drugs, sex, alcohol, porn, and money can provide a temporary high, but when it wears off you will want more. The world cannot satisfy the God shaped desire in your heart. God is the only One who provides eternal joy and peace and a life forever with Him in heaven. No matter where you go or how far you travel in life remember who your Father is. Even if you are going through a valley experience, Father God still shelters you.

10 Ways To Survive A Valley Experience

If God says no to our will, still say yes to His will. If we want something and God never gives it to us, still trust Him. God is so omniscient that if we got what we want we could be destroyed. God's will is much better than our will. Faith in God is belief that God will keep His promises. He says, He is with us, believe Him. He says, you will overcome, believe Him. You will survive a valley experience. Keep gripping to Jesus and don't let go.

A SECRET PLACE

A secret place is a good shelter in valley experiences. David says, "For in the time of trouble He shall hide me in His pavilion, in the secret place of His tabernacle He shall hide me; He shall set me high upon a rock" (Psalm 27:5). In the secret place of God the enemies cannot find you and the devil can do you no harm. Our Father is in the secret place with us and is protecting us from Satan. Many times, we must go to God in secret prayers and ask him for the things we need. Late in the midnight hour, we need to fall down on our knees and ask God for forgiveness. The secret place is for us to get alone with God and receive His power.

A hiding place

A hiding place is also a good shelter in a valley experience. David says in Psalm 32:7, "You are my hiding place; You shall preserve me from trouble; You shall surround me with songs of deliverance." In the hiding place you may see the devil coming, but he cannot find you because God has you hidden. David says, "Keep me as the apple of your eye; Hide me under the shadow of Your wings, from the wicked who oppress me, from my deadly enemies who surround me" (Psalm 17:8-9). God is always present in the hiding place and keeps us safe. Psalm 119:114 says, "You are my

Chapter 4: Key 4: Get Shelter

hiding place and my shield; I hope in Your word."

God had Moses in a hiding place when in Exodus 1:22 "Pharaoh commanded all his people saying, 'Every son who is born you shall cast into the river'". God had Jesus in a hiding place in Egypt when Herod sought to kill all male children 2 years old and under in Matthew 2:14-18. God does not hide us because He is afraid. God hides us because we are like babies - constantly needing His love, care, attention, and help. Now as believers, we are hidden with Christ. Colossians 3:3 states, "For you died, and your life is hidden with Christ in God." We are dead to sin and live to God by faith in Jesus. We are spiritually alive in Christ and crucify our fleshly desires to sin.

God hides us because He loves us so much. Without God, we are naked, corrupt, dirty, helpless, and in want. With God, we are covered with clean garments of love, praise, and righteousness. In the glorious future, saints will be clothed in white garments, incorruption, and immortality. 1 Corinthians 15:53 says, "For this corruptible must put on incorruption, and this mortal will put on immorality." God does not want people to die in a sinful body, but wants us to live forever with a glorified body that can never decay.

God hides us in the day of trouble and disastrous times. There is a judgment day also and God will have vengeance and recompense over rebellion, pride, idolatry, injustice, unbelief, blasphemy, immorality, wickedness, abomination, lying, iniquity, evil, and sin. God's wrath will be poured out on the entire earth and only we who are in Christ will be spared. God is saying to all, "Come out of her, my people, lest you share in her sins, and lest you receive of her plagues" (Revelation 18:4). We are to come out of the world's system and be hidden in Christ and we will be survivors. When we come out of the worldly methods we must leave everything negative behind. Do not take idols, fornication, evil, mischief, pride, uncleanness, manipulation, lust, lying, envy, jealousy, hate, and other wicked principles and immoral devices. Look to Jesus to give you a new life filled with love, righteousness, peace, joy, truth, faithfulness, light, and rewards.

Zephaniah 2:3 states, "Seek the Lord, all you meek of the earth, who have upheld His justice. Seek righteousness, seek humility. It may be that you will be hidden in the day of the Lord's anger." God is holy and just and He has to rightfully judge sin. Believers do not have to experience the wrath and condemnation of God because His wrath was poured out on Jesus on the cross. Joel prophesied, " The Lord also will roar from Zion, and utter His voice from Jerusalem; The heavens and earth will shake; But the Lord will be a shelter for His people, and the strength of the children of Israel" (Joel 3:16). We do not have to fear when the sorrow comes, because we are in the shelter of the Lord. Amos says, "Seek good and not evil, that you may live; so the Lord God of host will be with you, as you have spoken. Hate evil, love good; establish justice in the gate. It may be that the Lord God of hosts will be gracious to the remnant of Joseph" (Amos 5:14-15). We need to get shelter in God's hiding place. We cannot hide from God in our own strength, but we can hide in Christ. God still gives us time to repent. " The Lord is not slack concerning His promise, as some count slackness, but is longsuffering toward us, not willing that any should perish, but that all should come to repentance" (2 Peter 3:9). Repent, accept Christ today. If anyone goes to hell it is his or her own fault- not God's.

Chapter 4: Key 4: Get Shelter

A HEALING PLACE

A healing place is a good shelter in a valley experience. Psalm 147:2-3 states, "The Lord builds up Jerusalem; He gathers together the outcasts of Israel. He heals the brokenhearted and binds up their wounds." God is able and has healed all kinds of physical, family/social, financial, mental, emotional, mental, sexual, and spiritual sickness. Jesus Christ went about healing the sick and healing is available today. Peter says, "Who Himself bore our sins in His own body on the tree, that we having died to sins, might live for righteousness- by whose stripes you were healed" (1 Peter 2:24). The hands of Jesus are healing hands. The blood of Jesus is healing blood. God restores us to our health, right mind, and heals all wounds- even the self-inflicted ones. It is God's desire that we are healed (nothing broke, nothing missing, nothing lacking, nothing hurting, and nothing lost). Sickness and disease rise up against God's people because of Satan, disobedience, and the curse. We are healed from sickness and disease by faith in God's power. We pray for the sick, lay hands on the sick, and they will recover because miracles happen when we believe that Jesus is the Healer and Great Physician. The power of Christ is present to heal cancer, heart problems, leg problems, blood disease, kidney problems, female issues, male issues, vision, hearing, brain, mental disorder, emotional illness, diabetes, feet, organs, any issue. We must go to the healing place found only in the blood of Jesus. Isaiah 53:4 states, "Surely He has borne our griefs and carried our sorrows; yet we esteemed Him stricken, smitten by God, and afflicted. But He was wounded for our transgressions, He was bruised for our iniquities; the chastisement for our peace was upon Him and by His stripes we are healed." Good news: there is healing in Jesus. God made man in His image and we were originally created to live forever; however, the sin curse came in and people have been dying and getting sick since the time of Adam's disobedience. Jesus came to reverse the curse, and now we can have good health, wealth, and success in every area of our lives. Jesus Christ is the healing place – Get shelter.

A RESTING PLACE

A resting place is also a good shelter as you go through a valley experience. In a resting place we can relax, replenish, re-energize, and refresh. In the struggles and low places of life, we can get cranky, restless, and tired physically, mentally, and emotionally. We find rest for our souls in Jesus Christ. Jesus says, "Take My yoke upon you and learn from me, for I am gentle and lowly in heart, and you will find rest for your souls" (Matthew 11:29). We can rest even in a valley experience because God is in control.

To relax means to get in a state of ease and comfort. After a busy day at work or at home, it feels nice to take off our shoes and recline on a couch or our favorite chair. Likewise, we can rest in Jesus knowing that we are safe and secure in His arms. Times of relaxation are necessary even in a Christian's life because we need to release all of the negative pressures of life.

Also we need time of rest for replenishing and reenergizing. People give out and do not take in because they think it is all up to them; however, if people work and work and do not take a break, they will become unproductive. Life is not all about self anyway. Jesus told His disciples, "'Come aside, by yourselves to a deserted place and rest a

Chapter 4: Key 4: Get Shelter

while.' For there were many coming and going, and they did not have time to eat" (Mark 6:31). Jesus understood that the disciples needed to slow down and nourish their physical bodies as well as their soul and spirit. We need to take time to pray, read the Bible, rest, eat, sleep, laugh, and listen to the Holy Spirit. After spending time alone with Jesus, we will then gain the strength needed to continue the journey. Do not burn out while going through a valley experience. Let the Holy Spirit lead you to a resting place. You do not have to walk through the valley experience by yourself.

Also we need a resting place for refreshing. Refresh means to revive, recover, and rejuvenate. When we are persecuted, tried, tested, overlooked, talked about, lied on, and beaten down because we are living for Christ, we can become weary. In our weariness, we need God to refresh us and restore us back to His strength. Psalm 138:7 says, "Though I walk in the midst of trouble, you will revive me; You will stretch out your hand against the wrath of my enemies, and your right hand will save me." Psalm 80:17-19 says, "Let Your hand be upon the man of Your right hand, upon the son of man whom You made strong for yourself. Then we will not turn back from you; Revive us and we will call upon Your name, revive us, O Lord God of Hosts; cause Your face to shine, and we shall be saved!" When we enter God's resting place and get refreshed, we can shout for joy in the midst of perilous times and keep on believing in Jesus.

A HOLY PLACE

We find shelter to survive the valley experience, by going to God's Holy place. In God's Holy Place He covers us, protects us, and fights for us supernaturally. We have a supernatural birth and supernatural baptism in the Holy place. In John 3:5, "Jesus answered, Verily, verily, I say unto thee, except a man be born of water and of the Spirit, he cannot enter into the kingdom of God." To be born into the kingdom of God we must experience a spiritual birth. The supernatural birth of the spirit happens when believers come to Jesus. Jesus makes us new mentally, emotionally, and spiritually. We enter God's Holy place to learn and know our Father, praise and worship our Father, communicate with our Father, and get spiritual wisdom.

The supernatural baptism is the baptism in the Holy Ghost. When we get spiritually fire baptized, God burns away the things that hinder our spirits. Acts 2:38 says, "Then Peter said to them, Repent, and let every one of you be baptized in the name of Jesus Christ for the remission of sins, and you shall receive the gift of the Holy Spirit." The flesh wars against the spirit and the soul. Fasting keeps the flesh under submission unto the power of the Holy Spirit. Deny the flesh and feed the spirit. Your spirit wants God and the gifts of God, but the flesh wants earthly affections and lusts. Believers must receive the Holy Spirit and get into a Holy place. Ephesians 5:9-10 says, "(for the fruit of the Spirit is in all goodness, righteousness, and truth), finding out what is acceptable to the Lord." Sin is not okay unto God and it never will be. Instead of us trying to minimize the severity of any sin, we need to maximize the Sovereignty of the Holy Spirit and be under the control of God.

In the Old Testament, the priest had to come once a year to the Holy place to make sin offerings and burnt offerings for themselves and the people. In the New Testament, we have a new High Priest and sin offering which is Jesus

Chapter 4: Key 4: Get Shelter

Christ and His blood. Hebrews 9:11-12 says,

> "But Christ came as the High Priest of the good things to come with the greater and more perfect tabernacle not made with hands, that is, not of this creation. Not with the blood of goats and calves, but with His own blood He entered the Most Holy Place once for all, having obtained eternal redemption."

The only way we can enter into the Holy place is by the blood of Jesus where we have forgiveness of sin. In Jesus, there is redemption, salvation, holiness, forgiveness, righteousness, truth, love, justification, sanctification, remission, healing, renewing, rest, abundant living, and other good things.

No matter what you are going through – sickness, financial loss, mental and emotional depression, family disputes, spiritual valleys, etc. - we find shelter in God. God's arms are not too short that He cannot save. God's ears are not deaf and He hears our faintest cries. God's hands are not tied and He delivers us from the snare of the enemy. God's heart is not hardened and He forgives our sin. God's eyes are not blind and He sees our struggle. God's mouth is not muzzled and He speaks on our behalf. God's power is not limited and He works miracles. God is not dead and He is worthy of our praise. "I will say of the Lord, He is my refuge and my fortress; My God in Him I will trust" (Psalm 91:2). God's plan and thoughts for us are survival of valley experiences and exaltation. The Lord helps us to survive because we cannot make it out on our own. Get sheltered by God.

10 Ways To Survive A Valley Experience

CHAPTER 5
KEY 5: GET THE WORD

"Your word is a lamp to my feet and a light to my path."—Psalm 119:105

In the valley experience, you have to withstand sickness, addictions, temptations, Satan, depressions, low self-esteem, and spiritual warfare. You need a weapon and one combat weapon is the word of God. Apostle Paul admonishes believers to "put on the whole armor of God" found in Ephesians 6. In Ephesians 6:17 he says, "take the helmet of salvation and the sword of the Spirit, which is the word of God". God's word is very important to fight against the enemy. When Satan comes against you and your family, you need to have a word that will dispel any lie he is telling you. God's word is "living, powerful, and sharper than any two-edged sword, piercing even to the division of soul and spirit, and of joints and marrow, and is a discerner of the thoughts and intents of the heart" (Hebrews 4:12). God's word communicates, corrects, comforts, enlightens, exhorts, sanctifies, and cleanses.

THE WORD COMMUNICATES

God uses His word to communicate to His children. God's message tells His thoughts, will, plan, and redemption. Jeremiah reveals God's word in Jeremiah 29:11 saying, "For I know the thoughts I think toward you, says the Lord, thought of peace and not of evil, to give you a future and a hope." Thus, you may go through a valley but you must have a future and an expected arrival to greater things in God. Our hope is found in Christ. "All scripture of the Bible were given by inspiration of God and is profitable for doctrine, for reproof, for correction, for instruction in righteousness, that the man of God may be complete, throughly equipped for every good work" (2 Timothy 3:16-17). The word of God is good for everyone. God's will is stated in His word. His plan and redemptive will are stated in John 6:39-40, "This is the will of the Father who sent Me 'that of all He has given Me I should lose nothing, but should raise it up at the last day.' And this is the will of Him who sent Me 'that everyone who sees the Son and believe in Him may have everlasting life, and I will raise Him up at the last day.'" God is telling us in His word that we have salvation and resurrection in Jesus.

THE WORD CORRECTS

God's word corrects when we do things wrong or omit to do the things God said to do. When we hear a message, a prophecy, or read the Bible, we can then evaluate and rid the disobedience in our lives. Repent, and do better. Correction from God is necessary for unsaved and saved people. Unsaved people come to God and are made saved. Saved people come to God with a need for Him to improve

CHAPTER 5: KEY 5: GET THE WORD

our lives. When the word corrects us, it just means we need to do better. If God never told us that sin is wrong and we have to have faith in Jesus to be forgiven, we would still be lost. God exposes sin and provides a remedy for sin- the blood of Jesus. Without Jesus' blood, all would be lost, but because of the blood all have an opportunity for salvation. All who confess and believe in Jesus are saved regardless of race, creed, or gender. When corrected, we should make adjustments to our attitudes, ambitions, and/or backslidings. We do not practice sin and cannot make light of sin. Sin is like a weak man carrying a 12,000lb. weight on his spirit, soul, and body. Jesus lifts the heavy burden of sin and we no longer have to carry the weight of sin's condemnation and death. Romans 8:3-4 says, "For what the law could not do in that it was weak through the flesh, God did by sending his own Son in the likeness of sinful flesh, on the account of sin: He condemned sin in the flesh, that the righteous requirement of the law might be fulfilled in us who do not walk according to the flesh but according to the Spirit." Jesus carried our sin so that we can carry His righteousness.

THE WORD COMFORTS

Many times at memorial services a preacher gives "words of comfort" to a family. Words of comfort provide the family with the understanding of death and knowledge that the death is not the end of the person's life. It matters most how rich the person lives again when he or she dies in Christ. Nothing in this world can compare to eternal life with God- a life with no tears, no sorrows, no cares, no pain, no sickness, no death, no tragedy, no injustice, no crime, no hate, no fear, no sin, no curse, never goodbye,

10 Ways To Survive A Valley Experience

no darkness, no night, and no valley experiences. Heaven has already been prepared by God and is for believers in Jesus. Heavens' streets are paved with gold and have many precious jeweled foundations, but most of all God dwells there. If a man or woman lives and dies with God, he or she is rich. We need God more than anything or anyone. Spiritual death is separation from God because of the wickedness of the sin nature. God takes no pleasure in the death of wicked people. The Lord says to Ezekiel, "'Say to them, 'As I live', says the Lord God, I have no pleasure in the death of the wicked, but that the wicked turn from his way and live. Turn, turn from your evil ways! For why should you die, O house of Israel (33:11)?'" We find out in the word that believers may die physically, but never die spiritually. Believers experience riches from God on earth, in the spirit, and in heaven. God wants believers to prosper on earth, in the spirit, and in eternity.

> **Comforting scriptures for grieving families:**
>
> Psalm 116:15: "Precious in the sight of the Lord is the death of His saints."
>
> Isaiah 41:10: "Fear not, for I am with you, Be not dismayed, for I am your God. I will strengthen you, Yes, I will help you, I will uphold you with my righteous right hand."

In a valley experience, God's word comforts His children. The Psalms has great comforting scriptures such as in Psalm

CHAPTER 5: KEY 5: GET THE WORD

4:1, "Hear me when I call O God of my righteousness! You have relieved me in my distress." How comforting to know that God reassures us that He heals pains. Psalm 67:1 says, "God be merciful to us and bless us and cause His face to shine upon us." Psalm 27:1 says, "The Lord is the light of my salvation, whom shall I fear? The Lord is the strength of my life; of whom shall I be afraid?" Psalm 119:92 says, "Unless your law had been my delight, I would have perished in my affliction." When you are feeling depressed, God's word encourages you to hold on a little longer knowing that God will bring you out of the valley you are currently going through.

THE WORD ENLIGHTENS

God's word also enlightens His children in their valley experience. God's word is a lamp and a light. A light keeps us from darkness and falling into dark places. Jesus is the light of the world and He is the way out of the valley experiences. Micah 7:8 says, "Do not rejoice over me, my enemy; when I fall, I will arise; when I sit in darkness the Lord will be a light to me." Even in the darkest night or valley experience, Jesus (God's word made flesh) will light up the situation. The brightest light ever is Jesus Christ and if you accept Him as Lord and Savior and believe that He died and rose again for our sins you will be saved from darkness. Get the Word.

THE WORD EXHORTS

God's word also exhorts. Biblical exhortations are for inspiration and for cautions. The Bible teaches us to pray, confess Jesus as Lord and Savior, give thanks, give tithes and offerings, love others, take communion, fellowship with other believers, and receive the baptism of the Holy Spirit and other positives. The Bible also warns against sinful behaviors and tells us to live unto Jesus, resist the devil, and crucify the lust of the flesh. We have to make the decision to believe God's word, accept Christ, and receive eternal life or disbelieve God's word, reject Christ and receive eternal damnation. Heaven is for real and lasts for eternity and hell also is real and its' lake of fire burns for eternity. Jesus has already prepared a place for believers, so we need to continue on believing and always be ready for His return. As we learn better, we need to do better. As we learn better, we need to love better. As we learn better, we need to live, walk, and talk better. As we learn more, we also grow more. Warnings are not to shame individuals it is to improve our relationship with God. No one can say that they have no room for improvement and are incapable of making mistakes. All are continuously maturing as we go through valley experiences and endure life changes. God's word is vital for helping us to become what God intends us to be. Maturation is not based upon chronological age, but on personal experiences with God through Jesus Christ. God's word can encourage and warn. One person may need an encouraging word, but someone else may need a word of warning. Another person may need a word of confirmation. Another may need a prophetic word. Thank God for the Holy Spirit because He supplies pastors/preachers/ministers with messages of encouragement, warnings, confirmations, and /or prophecies in one sermon.

THE WORD SANCTIFIES

God's word sanctifies or sets us apart. We are different from the world because God's word is planted in the hearts of

Chapter 5: Key 5: Get The Word

Christians. Jesus says, "Sanctify them by your truth. Your word is truth" (John 17:17). The sinful world has accepted a lie that people can live how they want, and do what feels good and nothing bad is going happen to them. Believers have the truth that we must live holy and do what God speaks for we are saved by the blood of Jesus, and will live forever with God. We belong to God and when believers go through valley experiences, we remember God's word. Psalm 119:140-44 says,

> "Your word is very pure; therefore, Your servant loves it. I am small and despised, yet I do not forget Your precepts. Your righteousness is an everlasting righteousness, and your law is truth. Trouble and anguish have overtaken me, yet your commandments are my delights. The righteousness of Your testimonies is everlasting; Give me understanding and I shall live."

It's okay to be different from the world; you are following God's command. Obey God even if your family, friends, co-workers, or peers are pressuring you to sin. You may lose friendships or relationships, but God's way is narrow and right. Psalm 119:160 says, "The entirety of Your word is truth, and every one of Your righteous judgments endure forever." Even if you get criticized because of your faith in Christ you will get a reward.

THE WORD CLEANSES

God's word cleans us and washes us and makes us pure. Jesus says in John 15:3, "You are already clean because of the word which I have spoken to you." David says in Psalm

51:7, "Purge me with hyssop, and I shall be clean; wash me, and I shall be whiter than snow." Isaiah says in Isaiah 1:18, "'Come now, and let us reason together', says the Lord, 'Though your sins are like scarlet, they shall be as white as snow; though they are red like crimson, they shall be as wool.'" Jesus Christ is the washer of our sins and we can be spotless in God's eyes. We are clean if we hear, understand, believe, and live out God's word. We must keep God's word in our hearts, in our souls, in our spirits, on our minds, on our lips, in our ears, before our eyes, and in our actions continually. We cannot ignore God's word if we are going to survive valley experiences.

GET THE WORD

To get God's word in your heart, you have to read the Bible and meditate on the scriptures. Additionally, you can go to church, watch Christian television programs, go to Sunday school, go to Bible classes, and Bible study. The world has its own systems and words and ideas. God's systems, words, and ideas are right and are far better than any worldly religion. I recommend that you purchase the Holy Bible, and start reading Old Testament and New Testament scriptures. If you do not understand the Bible, pray to God and ask the Holy Spirit to make it clearer. Also, attend Church so an apostle, pastor, teacher, prophet or evangelist will feed you with more knowledge and understanding.

DO THE WORD

It's not good just to read and hear God's word letting it go in one ear and out the other. We must study the word, believe the word, and do what the word is communicating. It is hard to "let not your heart be troubled" (John 14:1a)

CHAPTER 5: KEY 5: GET THE WORD

in valley experiences, but all of God's words are true! In a struggle with depression, take your mind off the situation and trust in God that He accomplishes all things written in His word. When I take my focus off the problem, I find the solution written in God's Holy Bible. God may not fix the problem when we think He should, but His word is always on time. Blessings come to those who hear and do God's word without doubting and disbelief. Sometimes you will have to wait on the answer, but the answer is guaranteed. Trials will come, but victory comes with getting God's word and having faith in Jesus.

THE HOLY SPIRIT

Jesus promised a comforter which is the Holy Spirit. The Holy Spirit hears, teaches, and speaks God's word and brings it to our memory. The Holy Spirit speaks to our human spirit telling us that these are only temporal afflictions and valleys we go through. They are not everlasting. He gives us peace and joy in the midst of the storm. The Holy Spirit gives prophetic words according to 2 Peter 1:20-21, "knowing this first, that no prophecy of scripture is of any private interpretation, for prophecy never came by the will of man, but holy men of God spoke as they were moved by the Holy Spirit." Jesus said in John 14:26. "But the Helper, the Holy Spirit, whom the Father will send in My name, He will teach you all things and bring to your remembrance all things that I said to you." The Holy Spirit dwells in believers by faith, and comforts us in any valley experience and reminds us of all the promises of God revealed by and through Jesus Christ.

THE LIVING WORD

God's word is alive and brings life to hearers, doers, and believers. Psalm 119:50 says, "This is my comfort in my affliction, for Your word has given me life." Everything written in the Bible comes from God and is applicable to any valley you may be going through. Jesus Christ is the living Word. Valley experiences teach us that the one being we cannot live without is God. God gives us strength, word, breath, and life. "He answered and said, 'it is written, Man shall not live by bread alone, but by every word that proceeds from the mouth of God'" (Matthew 4:4).

Come to Jesus, He gives food and drink to hungry and thirsty souls – His body and His blood. We need deliverance- it's in the Word. We need peace- it's in the Word. We need salvation- it's in the Word. We need hope- it's in the Word. We need healing- it's in the Word. We need joy- it's in the Word. We need love- it's in the Word. We need comfort- it's in the Word. We need life- it's in the Word. We need prosperity- it's in the Word. The Word of God (Jesus) equips us with everything we need for survival and victory. God's Word gives us faith to endure hardships, overcome anxieties, and face the challenges of life joyfully.

HAVE FAITH IN THE WORD YOU HEAR

We begin to have faith as we go to church and start to hear God's word and believe it. Men and women of God have been anointed to preach, teach, evangelize, prophesy, and proclaim God's words. Romans 10:17 says, "So then faith comes by hearing, and hearing by the word of God." As we believe the words of God and believe that God is speaking through individuals we know that no earthly person wrote the Bible. You can never get tired of hearing the word and never stop learning the word of God. The Holy Bible is

CHAPTER 5: KEY 5: GET THE WORD

God centered, God inspired, God created, God spoken, and God authored. There are many translations, but one message to all – Jesus saves.

WISDOM OF THE WORD

God's word has wisdom. Proverbs is a great book of wisdom that gives us practical advice for godly living, wise counsel, training children, joyful marriages, being competent in the workplace and living in our communities, neighborhoods, and homes. He who is wise will read Proverbs in the midst of a valley experience. Also, Psalms is a great book of prayers, songs, praises, worship, and prophecy. Many contemporary gospel music hits have their roots in the book of Psalms. There are 150 numbers of Psalms and the majority of them give praise and worship to God in a song format. Both the Old and New Testament scriptures are filled with stories, principles, and words to benefit us today. It is very advantageous for a person to get the word whether they are in the valley, coming out the valley, or on the way into a valley. The word of God is good in all seasons of your life. God's Bible stands against the test of time and has been quoted more than any other book because it is real, relevant, and not outdated. Get God's word- it is very wise, practical, powerful, useful, enlightening, comforting, correcting, cleaning, sanctifying, and life-giving.

WHAT TO DO WITH THE WORD?

We must hear, understand, read, speak, believe, and do God's word. If we only hear the word and not believe it, we are unfruitful people. Consider Luke 8:15, "But the ones that fell on the good ground are those who having heard the word with a noble and good heart, keep it and bear fruit with patience." In a valley experience, Satan tries to make us disobey or discredit God's word, but we must not follow Satan's distractions. Satan is a liar, deceiver, destroyer, and thief. Satan twists God's word to fit his agenda and attempts to deceive the elect of God. We should pray and ask God to give us an understanding of His word and give us spiritual discernment of false prophets. And, we need to go to churches where pastors and preachers preach the un-compromised and true word of God. Apostles, pastors, teachers, evangelist, and prophets have gifts from God to explain the word better so people can understand it. Pastors study the word extensively to say what God has spoken and to rightly divide the word.

GOD'S WORDS HAVE POWER

God's words have the power to draw unbelievers to salvation and sinners to repentance. Isaiah 55:11 says, "So shall My word be that goes forth from My mouth; It shall not return to Me void, but it shall accomplish what I please, and it shall prosper in the thing for which I send it." God sent His word to heal, save, and deliver us. God sent His Word (which is Jesus Christ) and if Jesus Christ abides in us we can survive valley experiences. God is not a man that lies, and whatever He says He will bring it to existence.

GOD'S WORD REVEALS HIMSELF

Throughout the Bible, from Genesis unto Revelation, God reveals His names, character, skill, nature, power, divinity, and love for humanity. God is:

God, Creator, Provider, Yahweh, Jehovah, Spirit, Instructor, Lord, Maker, Most High, Friend, Almighty,

CHAPTER 5: KEY 5: GET THE WORD

Wisdom, Deliverer, Shelter, My banner, Present Help, Holy, Jealous God, Righteous, Justice, Mercy, Grace, Love, Faithful, Redeemer, Truth, One, The Lord Your God, Rock, Salvation, Conqueror, Savior, Living God, Alpha and Omega, Judge, King, Father, Healer, The Portion of Jacob, God of the Universe, Ancient of Days, Avenger, Eternal, Everlasting King, Lord God of Israel, Perfect, Lord God of Abraham, Isaac, and Israel, Comforts, Consuming Fire, Our Refuge, Sovereign, Omnipresent, YAH, Omniscience, Power, Light, God-Who-Forgives, Good Shepherd, Bishop, Strength, Shield, King of glory, King of kings, Lord of lords, Strong Tower, Fortress, Good, Safety, Master, Hope, Exceeding Joy, Great, Mighty One, Awesome, Holy One of Israel, God of hosts, Godhead, Well-beloved, Most Upright, Majesty, High and Lofty One, Potter, Living God, The Lord our Righteousness, Ruler, Abba, Righteous Father, Holy Father, God in Christ, God of our Lord Jesus Christ, Father of glory, God of Peace, The Holy One, God our Savior, Dayspring, Messiah, Lawgiver, The Father, the Word, the Holy Spirit, Lord God Almighty, I Am Who I Am, Mighty One, King of the saints, Lord God Omnipotent, Lord God Himself, Divine Nature, Possessor of heaven and earth, Keeper, Shade, The fountain of living waters, Mighty God, and many more wonderful titles.

GOD'S WORD IS SUPREME

Get God's word and let God's word reign in your heart, mind, actions, and life. The decisions you make have consequences, so choose wisely. These are the consequences for fellowship with Satan: death, hell, separation, the lake of fire and brimstone, eternal damnation. There is a reward for a relationship with Jesus (abundant life, love, heaven, adoption, eternal life, rest). God sent His Word to us so we can have life in Christ Jesus, His Son. Valley experiences can be survived if God's Word is with us and in us. God is our Hope and Strength and we lean and depend on Him totally. God's word tells believers who we are in Christ Jesus: more than conquerors, beloved, blessed, righteous, holy, blameless, above reproach, sons, His servants, pardoned, favored, qualified, kings and priests, worthy, rich, overcomers, faithful, loved, perfect, saints, redeemed, disciples, victorious, chosen, called, His people, witnesses, saved, alive, healed, children of light, heirs, justified, clean, sheep, slaves of righteousness, sober, vigilant, a new creation, ambassadors, righteousness of God in Him, strong, sanctified, a peculiar people, accepted in the Beloved, adopted, a holy nation, the people of God, enriched, precious and many more.

CHAPTER 6

KEY 6: PRAISE YOUR WAY THROUGH

"I will bless the Lord at all times; His praise shall continually be in my mouth."—Psalm 34:1

Praise God, even in a valley experience. Praise means to admire, worship, and give great reverence to. We praise the Lord at all times because God is our Creator, Deliverer, Healer, and Provider. Without God we are nothing and we can do nothing without God. We exist because God has made us, and breathed in us the breath of life. God always is and always will be. The psalmist says, "Let everything that has breath Praise the Lord "(Psalm 150:6). So, if you are still breathing do not stop giving God praise.

PRAISE THROUGH THE VALLEY

So, why praise in a valley experience? Because God is Creator, He is all knowing. God knows all about us- physically, mentally, financially, family/socially, emotionally, spiritually, sexually, educationally, etc. God will not allow us to go through something that will kill us, so we praise our Creator. If the load is too heavy for us to bear, He steps right on in and carries us through. Psalm 50:23 says, "Whoever offers praise glorifies Me, and to him who orders his conduct aright, I will show the salvation of God."

God is our Deliverer. When you are at the lowest point, God delivers you into a place of shelter, security, and safety. Praise the Lord, O my soul who deliverers me from the valley of the shadow of death. In the Bible, God delivered the children of Israel out of Egypt, He delivered Daniel out of the lion's den, and He delivered Shadrach, Meshach, and Abednego from the fiery furnace. These biblical accounts have two things in common: 1st- they went in, 2nd they came out safe. Therefore, you may go in the valley experiences, but you will come out safe if God is on your side. Psalm 34:19 says, "Many are the afflictions of the righteous, but the Lord delivers him out of them all." Even if you are in a valley, you will be delivered.

God is our Healer. Isaiah 53:5 says, "But He was wounded for our transgression, He was bruised for our iniquities, that chastisement for our peace was upon Him, and by His stripes we are healed." We are healed in Jesus. I praise God because there is no sickness He cannot heal. To receive God's healing power, we must have faith that God heals all sickness and disease. God does not punish His children with sickness and disease. He wants all healed. Sickness and disease came about because Adam disobeyed God in the garden and healing came about because Jesus obeyed God and gave up His life that we might be set free. Romans 5:19 says, "For as by one man's disobedience many were made sinners, so also by one Man's obedience many will be

Chapter 6: Key 6: Praise Your Way Through

made righteous." We have the right to healing, wellness, and life by the blood of Jesus. Praise the Lord!

God is our Provider. Philippians 4:19 says, "And My God shall supply all your need according to His riches in glory by Christ Jesus." God is the richest being alive and provides believers with an abundance of blessings. Even if you lose your job, have no money in the bank, and seem to be in a worst financial state – Praise the Lord anyhow. God provides by sending someone to help or causing you to receive an unexpected financial blessing. Do not lose hope and do not get depressed if you do not have money. Jesus says in Matthew 6:25 "… do not worry about your life, what you will eat or what you will drink, nor about your body what you will put on, is not life more than food and the body more than clothing?" If we seek God and His ways of doing, He supplies the things we need. The righteous will not be abandoned in difficult times, and do not lack for anything when the world is in financial ruin. God knows what we need and He provides our every need- Praise the Lord!

WHEN TO PRAISE

So, when do we praise the Lord? At all times, we praise the Lord. In pain, in sickness, in glad times, in joyful times, in sad times, in the morning, in the noonday, in the night, on the weekend, through the weekdays, and in the valley experiences; we praise the Lord. God is worthy of praise every second, every minute, 24 hours a day, 7 days a week, and 365 days a year. I praise God for my past, present, and future. I praise God for my past because I know that all things that happened good or bad "worked together for good to those who love God, to those who are the called according to His purpose" (Romans 8:28). I praise God for my present, because I know that God Himself has said, "I will never leave nor forsake you" (Hebrews 13:5). I praise God for my future because "Jesus Christ is the same yesterday, today, and forever" (Hebrews 13:8). At all times, God is giving us His breath, life, forgiveness, grace, and mercy. Yes, we praise God even in a valley experience knowing that God allows us to survive the valley. Praise the Lord- we outlived what tried to destroy us.

HOW TO PRAISE

So, how do we praise the Lord? We praise with our whole heart, mouth, voice, hands, feet, and soul. We sing songs of praise, clap our hands, use instruments, dance, shout, cry out extols, lift our hands, and others. In the church we say, "Holy, Glory, Amen, Thank You Jesus, Glory to God, Hallelujah, Praise the Lord," and others. Praise the Lord faithfully, publicly, and privately. In the Bible, giving of tithes and offerings is considered praise. In the Bible, David offered God a sacrifice and praise. "Then David danced before the Lord with all his might…." So David and all the house of Israel brought up the ark of the Lord with shouting and with the sound of the trumpet" (2 Samuel 6:14-15). Do not be concerned with who sees you in the natural when you praise; the important purpose is that God sees and hears and He gets the glory. All of our praise and worship is for God and there are many ways to praise.

IN ALL THINGS GIVE THANKS

In all things give thanks for we still see God's uplifting hand in the unpleasant situations too. If you have no friends, what a friend you have in Jesus. If you lose your job, God

Chapter 6: Key 6: Praise Your Way Through

is your source. If your children misbehave, children are a blessing from God. If your husband/wife divorces you, God is with you always. If your house is foreclosed on, God is your shelter. If a loved one dies, there is eternal life in Jesus. If you get a bad diagnosis, you are healed by the stripes of Jesus. If the summers are hot and the winters are cold, God is the God of the whole earth. If you are lonely and have no spouse, God is changing you into a virtuous woman or godly man. If your elderly parents' strength is weakening, even in old age and weakness God is present and strong on their behalf. If your child is born with a physical or mental disability, God looks at the heart and he or she is still blessed. If you are in a valley experience, God brings you through with a testimony. We do not understand the bad and undesired things that happen in our lives, but we still can give thanks to God because even on the darkest night God's light still shines in our lives.

BENEFITS OF PRAISE

Some of the benefits of praise for believers are breakthrough, blessings, bountifulness, and buoyancy:

Breakthrough. In the valley, it may seem that you are about to lose everything, including your sanity. In the world, some people have suffered a nervous breakdown. Hate filled people do and say things that make us upset. Satan and his demonic forces attack and try to steal our joy. Instead of falling apart, I say have a breakthrough. Breakthrough is a coming forth and a step onward in the direction toward Jesus. Praise your way through all the mental, physical, and emotional pain. Sometimes we face challenges or valleys we wish we could avoid, but God gives us the strength to make it through. Do not break down and stay in a valley experience because you feel low. Hold your head up and look up and praise your way through. Breakthrough is on the other side of the valley. When a woman experiences childbirth, the birthing process is painful; however, when the labor is complete, she delivers a beautiful baby and rejoices that her child is born into the world. Praise the Lord!

Blessings. "When praises go up, blessings come down" is a phrase that I often hear at church. As I draw closer to Christ, I see it is absolutely true. When I give God glory in the midst of life's valleys, I see God's blessing every day. He wakes me up, heals my body, saved my soul, gives me strength, restores my joy, makes me righteous, and pours blessings upon me – even when I don't deserve them. Blessings come in many shapes and sizes. The greatest blessing ever given was "wrapped up in swaddling clothes and laid in a manger" (Luke 2:7). Jesus was not born in a fancy hotel or hospital—He was born in a stable. Jesus was born in a lowly place, where animals were kept. I imagine, Mary and Joseph (His earthly parents) were praising God in spite of where they were. They forgot all about where they were located and were thankful to God for Jesus. What a great blessing for them to be a part of God's great plan of salvation. Praise the Lord!

Bountifulness. Praising the Lord also causes bountifulness in the valley experiences. God increases our joy, finance, health, family unity, and love because God is the God of more than enough. If we praise God and thank Him for what we do have, He causes us to get more of the blessings we need and even gives us some of the things we want. God

Chapter 6: Key 6: Praise Your Way Through

multiplies. Deuteronomy 7:13 states,

> "And He will love you and bless you and multiply you, He will also bless the fruit of your womb and the fruit of your land, your grain and your new wine and your oil, the increase of your cattle and the offspring of your flock in the land which He swore to your fathers to give you."

In modern terms, God is generous, and gives us the power to get wealth, our children to be blessed, and our businesses to thrive. So, when can we have this bountifulness? Right now and even if you are going through a valley. In prison, Paul wrote, "Rejoice in the Lord always, again I will say rejoice" (Philippians 4:23). Even when the outward circumstance is low, our inward perspective is high because we know God is the God of bountiful blessings. Praise the Lord!

Buoyancy. You may have gotten laid off from your job. When bills start piling high, you have a pain in your body, and you are feeling that you are drowning in a sorrowful pit of despair, praise the Lord. You are still alive and God will not let you drown. Buoyancy means capable for floating, happiness, and springiness. Buoyant people praise the Lord even when trouble is all around. God will keep you afloat in a valley experience because we praise Him and He loves us so much. The devil thought he could make you give up on God, but his plan did not work. Instead of sinking, you learned to call on the name of Jesus and He is anchoring your soul. In Acts Chapter 27 Paul is involved in a shipwreck, but he and the people on the ship with him survived. An angel had appeared to Paul and told him that he and all who sailed with him were going to arrive at the destination safely. In summary, Apostle Paul was on a ship with other prisoners, a storm came, and the prisoners and the guards were fearful. Paul tells the men to stay in the ship to be saved. The ship broke into pieces, and Paul and the rest were saved, just as Paul has spoken. Acts 27:44 says, "… and the rest, some on boards and some on parts of the ship, and so it was that they all escaped safely to land." God was with Paul and is also with us every step of the way. We survive because we give God glory and praise in the storm. After the storm is over we continue to give thanks to God. When the storm of life is raging, remember to praise the Lord. Praise is like a buoy and if your hold on to your praise God gives you the encouragement and support you need to survive and make it out of a valley experience.

PRAISE THE LORD!

"While I live I will praise the Lord; I will sing praise to my God while I have my being" (Psalm 146:2). Even in momentary outward brokenness, I will praise the Lord for His inward healing, blessing, and wholeness in the inner man. The outward blessings are on the way. Coming soon, the valley will be over and the victory will be realized. Do not let past failures, prevent present praise. Do not let your present circumstances cripple your praise. Do not let satanic attacks steal your praise. Do not let distractions detour your praise. Do not let mistakes mute your praise. Do not let hurt hinder your praise. Do not let heartbreak halt your praise. Do not let pain, pause your praise. We have the right, the reason, and the responsibility to praise God no matter what valley experience we go through. God is great,

Chapter 6: Key 6: Praise Your Way Through

good, generous, and a giving Father. Do praise Him in the morning and praise Him all day long. We can say thank you God for the battles we win, and the victories we have in Jesus Christ. As we praise God, we create an atmosphere for miracles to happen, pains to leave, deliverance to occur, chains to be broken, and blessings to come down from heaven. Let's continue to praise God at all times. Do not let a valley experience stop you from praising and worshiping the Living God. Take your praise off lay-a-way and give God some praise today. Sometimes, we unwisely want to wait until everything in our lives is picture-perfect and then we will start to praise the Lord. We want perfect health, perfect money in the bank, perfect jobs, perfect marriages, perfect churches, perfect families, perfect cars, perfect houses, perfect weather, etc. Jesus wants believers to praise Him even while going through a valley experience. Praise Him in advance. Praise God to give Him Exaltation and Glory. Praise the Lord!

10 Ways To Survive A Valley Experience

Chapter 7
KEY 7: PRAY

"And whatever things you ask in prayer, believing you will receive."—Matthew 21:22

While going through the valley experience, you may be looking for someone to talk to. Friends, family, pastors, counselors, and doctors can offer some encouragement or advice. Still, the greatest source of inspiration, counsel, and conversation is with God through prayer. And when you talk with God privately, He gives you the right answers and won't discuss your problems with anyone else.

PRAY

Prayer means to request or plead or to ask respectfully. Also, it involves giving thanks to God. Prayer is begging God to deliver you from a circumstance or give you the strength to endure the circumstance. When you pray to God, be specific about what you are asking Him for. If you need healing, ask. If you need, help, ask. If you need money, ask. If you need a miracle, ask. If you need a job, ask. If you need a spouse, ask. In all areas (physical, mental, emotional, sexual, financial, social, family, marital, educational, governmental, school, spiritual, etc.), pray about things. Prayer is a two-way street. We ask God for what we want and need and He reveals to us the things He wants from us or needs us to do. 2 Chronicles 7:14 says, "If My people who are called by My name will humble themselves, and pray and seek My face, and turn from their wicked ways, then I will hear from heaven, and will forgive their sins and heal their land." God hears what we pray for and is willing to give it to us if we repent and turn from our evil ways. America still has a chance to repent and turn away from wickedness. If we ask God to heal America and sincerely mean it, God will take us back to the humility, unity, moral lifestyles, and brotherly love that this nation was founded upon.

WHEN TO PRAY

So, when should I pray? The Bible says, "Pray without ceasing" (I Thessalonians 5:17). Do not go a day without praying to God, even if you do not feel like praying. Sometimes you may feel you have done so many things bad or wrong that God won't even hear your prayers. But, Jesus died for imperfect humans. And all sins are forgiven once you have accepted the Lord Jesus as the pardon of your sins. At the moment of salvation, you are no longer a sinner, you are now saved. God hates the sin, but He still loves sinners. Pray when things are going well, pray when things are bad. Even while going through a valley experience, pray and give thanks because God is delivering you.

HOW TO PRAY

Chapter 7: Key 7: Pray

So, how should I pray? Jesus disciples asked Him to teach them how to pray. In Luke 11:2-4 the model prayer is written:

> "He said to them, 'When you pray, say:
> 'Our father in heaven
> Hallowed be your name
> Your kingdom come
> Your will be done
> On earth as it is in heaven.
> Give us day by day our daily bread.
> And forgive us our sins,
> For we also forgive everyone who is indebted to us.
> And do not lead us into temptation
> But deliver us from the evil one.'"

Prayers give God glory, accept His will, ask for provision, ask for forgiveness, ask for protection, and always give thanks. Always pray from your heart and spirit and believe that God is able to do what you pray for.

God shows us how to pray. Matthew 6:5-9 says,

> "And when you pray you shall not be like the hypocrites. For they love to pray standing in the synagogues and on the corners of the streets, that they may be seen by men. Assuredly, I say to you, they have their reward. But you, when you pray, go into your room, and when you have shut your door, pray to your Father who is in the secret place; and your Father who sees in secret will reward you openly. And when you pray, do not use vain repetitions as the heathen do. For they think that they will be heard

for their many words. Therefore do not be like them; for your Father knows the things you have need of before you ask Him."

Jesus goes on to teach us that we pray and ask in His name. The Lord teaches us to pray for ourselves and others with a pure and truthful intention. Although God already knows what we need, we give Him extra latitude to work on our and others behalf when we pray. God does not need our permission to work all things out for us, but I think He wants us to know and believe that nobody but the Lord can do impossible things. When the doctor or lawyer says nothing else can be done, He says yes. God works best in believers whose spirits, hearts, minds, and wills are faithfully submitted to God's heart, mind, will, and Holy Spirit. God grants our petitions and we should give Him glory when our prayers are answered.

WHERE TO PRAY

So, where do we pray? Pray in the synagogue or church. God says His house is called the "house of prayer". Isaiah 56:7 says ... "for my house shall be called a house of prayer for all nations." God wants us to pray anywhere and always. Pray at home, at school, driving a car, at work, or where ever you may be. You may not be able to pray out loud, but your heart and spirit can make requests unto God. The devil was so upset about praying at school that it has been banned in many states; however, parents please pray for your children and teach them how to pray because God has the power to keep children safe. Even if you are in a hospital room, nursing facility, or jail cell do not forget to pray. Pray for salvation, safety, deliverance, healing, wisdom, help, living

Chapter 7: Key 7: Pray

holy, forgiveness, etc.

TYPES OF PRAYER

There are many types of prayer in the Bible. Here are a few types of prayers: prayers of supplication, confessions, faith, in the Spirit, intercession, thanksgiving, dedication, and agreement.

Prayers of supplication. Supplication is an intense prayer for God's divine favor. I Kings 8:45 says, "...then hear in heaven their prayer and their supplication and maintain their cause." God reveals secrets when we pray. When faced with a difficult task to interpret the king's dream or die physically, Daniel prayed that he might seek mercies from the God of heaven concerning this secret. God granted his request. In captivity, Daniel prayed with fasting. Daniel 9:3 states, "set my face toward the Lord God to make a request by prayers and supplications, with fasting, sackcloth, and ashes." God gave Daniel answers and understanding. Prayer and fasting destroy demonic oppressions. Pray for one another.

Prayers of confession. A confession acknowledges our sins and wrong doings and asks God for His abundant mercy. Prayers of confession are also used to confess Jesus as Lord and Savior of one's life. We acknowledge sin, confess Jesus, repent, and turn to God. God is merciful to everyone who calls on Him for the forgiveness of sin. Also, we must not hold any grudges against our fellow man, and forgive them of their sins against us. Denying the sin will not fix the problem. Admit it, repent, change the behavior, and go forward to living a life that is pleasing in the eyes of God.

10 Ways To Survive A Valley Experience

Prayer of faith. James 5:15 says, "And the prayer of faith will save the sick and the Lord will raise him up, and if he has committed sins, he will be forgiven." A prayer of faith is acknowledging trust in God to heal valley experiences: physical challenges, mental illness, sexual sin, emotional issues, financial lack, family divisions, etc. Psalm 50:15 says, "Call upon me in the day of trouble; I will deliver you and you shall glorify me." Faith is important because God is faithful to those who call upon the name of Jesus. Because Jesus is the way, the truth, and the life we go to God in prayer by faith in the name of Jesus. If you are in a valley of sickness, pray a prayer of faith knowing and believing that God has promised to heal in His word. Thank God for what He has done and wait for the manifestation. Sometimes you may or may not see immediate results in your condition, but the healing is already in your soul and body the moment you pray and receive the healing.

Prayer in the Spirit. Sometimes you may not be able to verbalize what you are praying for; however, God has given believers His Holy Spirit to help us pray. Romans 8:26 states, "Likewise the Spirit also helps in our weakness, For we do not know what we should pray for as we ought but the Spirit Himself makes intercession for us with groanings which cannot be uttered." Praying in the Spirit surpasses human intellect and understanding and goes beyond our limited speech unto a source of Power far exceeding our expectations. The Holy Spirit speaks directly to the God Head who is working on our behalf to interpret our groaning and heart cries. God understands even if we cannot because God knows our weaknesses, experiences, and position. God knows how to answer the call.

Chapter 7: Key 7: Pray

Prayers of intercession. To intercede means to plead for or on behalf of someone else or to pray in place of that person. In the valley, you can get prayers of intercession from your church, family, friends, pastors, and prayer lines. The greatest source of intercession is Jesus Christ who is currently making intercessions for us. You will survive the valley experience because God cares and people care enough to pray for one another. Also, you can intercede for someone else. James 5:16 says, "Confess your trespasses to one another, and pray for one another, that you may be healed. The effective, fervent prayer of a righteous man avails much." It is advantageous to pray for others and yourself. We need to intercede for sinful people, sick family members, neighboring world leaders, our government, our community, our world, church members, co-workers, children, parents, friends, etc. When people do not have the faith to believe God, we can pray that God will open their eyes of understanding so that they can pray for themselves in addition to our prayers for them.

Prayers of thanksgiving. In surviving the valley experience, offer to God prayers of thanksgiving because as you know- He is the source of survival. Thank God for your food, money, tithes, health, family, spouse, friends, etc. In everything, we give thanks because we appreciate the kindness of God. In John 6:11 when God fed the multitude Jesus gave thanks, "And Jesus took the loaves, and when He had given thanks, He distributed them to the disciples, and the disciples to those sitting down; and likewise of the fish, as much as they wanted." It is important to give thanks for the little because greater is coming. At times, things may happen to you that are not good or ideal, but still be thankful in the midst of trials and tribulations. Satan wants to lure believers away from God, so he can destroy us. We must continue to seek Jesus, pray, praise, worship, and survive.

Prayers of dedication. In 1 Kings 8:28-29 , King Solomon finished building the temple of the Lord and he prayed a prayer of dedication : "Yet regard the prayer of your servant and his supplication, O Lord My God, and listen to the cry and the prayer which your servant is praying before you today: that your eyes may be open toward this temple night and day, toward the place of which You said, 'My name shall be there that you may hear the prayer which Your servant makes toward this place.'" To dedicate means that something is being given to another for use. "Dedication" also means "to devote, consecrate, or to set apart as holy." In the New Testament Paul concludes that our body is "the temple of the Holy Spirit who is in you, whom you have from God, and you are not your own" (1 Corinthians 6:19). Also, Paul says in Romans 12:1, "I beseech you, therefore, brethren by the mercies of God that you present your bodies a living sacrifice, Holy, acceptable to God, which is your reasonable service." Since our bodies/temples belong to God we should dedicate ourselves to God. When praying, tell God that He is our owner. When going through a low place tell God I need You to survive. When we dedicate ourselves to God we understand that the totality of life consists of being pleasing to God- not oneself.

Prayers of agreement. Also, there is prayer of agreement. Jesus said in Matthew 18:19, "Again I say to you if two of you agree on earth concerning anything that they ask, it will be

Chapter 7: Key 7: Pray

done for them by My father in heaven." Corporate prayer and partner prayer bombards heaven and unites faith and believers to receive what they ask for according to God's will. Churches, families, couples, co-workers, schools, etc. need to pray in agreement.

NOTABLE PRAYERS IN THE BIBLE

Prayer resonates throughout the Bible. Four notable individual prayers really stand out: Hezekiah, Daniel, Hannah, and Jesus. From these prayers, we learn the impact of prayer and how we can use prayer in our lives today.

King Hezekiah prayed. King Hezekiah seemed to have it all together financially, emotionally, mentally, social/family, physical, etc. He was flourishing in the kingdom, had great wealth, prayed for others, and kept the laws of God joyfully. 2 Chronicles 31:21 says, "And in every work that he began in the service of the house of God, in the law and in the commandments, to seek his God, he did it with all his heart, so he prospered." But Hezekiah became sick and almost died and "he prayed to the Lord and he spoke to him and gave him a sign" (2 Chronicles 32:24). Hezekiah knew to ask God for healing and restoration. 2 Kings 20:2-3 says, "Then he turned his face toward the wall and prayed to the Lord saying, 'Remember now, O Lord I pray, how I have walked before You in truth and with a loyal heart, and have done what was good in your sight.' And Hezekiah wept bitterly." God heard his prayer and saw his tears, healed him and added more years to Hezekiah's life. 2 Kings 20:6 says, "'And I will add to your days fifteen years. I will deliver you and this city from the hand of the king of Assyria, and I will defend this city for my own sake, and for the sake of my servant David.'" Because Hezekiah humbled himself and prayed, God healed him from sickness. God gave Hezekiah further peace, healing, and God was a defense of the city. Likewise, God heals, delivers, defends, save, and adds years to our lives.

Daniel prayed. Daniel's prayers can be found in the book of Daniel. Daniel was greatly beloved by God and when Daniel prayed God gave him understanding of times, visions, dreams, and prophecy. Daniel prayed for kings, his government, countrymen, city, and for corporate forgiveness of the nation. In Daniel 9:16 he prays, " O Lord, according to all Your righteousness, I pray, let your anger and Your fury be turned away from Your city Jerusalem Your holy mountain; because for our sins, and for the iniquities of our fathers, Jerusalem, and Your people are a reproach to all those around us." Daniel had a global mindset in his prayers and was interceding on the behalf of others. God is a universal God and He prevents disaster from happening in the world if believers pray selflessly. Also, God reveals to Daniel a coming eternal kingdom. Daniel 2:44 says, "And in the days of these kings, the God of heaven will set up a kingdom which shall never be destroyed; and the kingdom shall not be left to other people; it shall break in pieces and consume all these kingdoms, and it shall stand forever." Jesus is King of Kings and He will rule in a future perfect kingdom and no saint will ever die in His kingdom. Everything in the natural realm is temporal and subject to change in time. Daniel 2:21-22 says, "And He [God] changes the times and the seasons; He removes kings and raises up kings; He gives wisdom to the wise and knowledge to those who have understanding. He reveals deep and secret

Chapter 7: Key 7: Pray

things; He knows what is in the darkness, and light dwells with Him." The valley experience is temporary and a good change is on the way, so continue to pray to God while you are going through. Daniel continued to pray even while he was in captivity and serving foreign people. Daniel had lows and had to wait for answers, but God always answered his prayers right on time. Daniel continuously prayed and gave thanks to God so He gave him wisdom and favor causing Daniel to advance in the kingdom. A delay is not denial. Keep on praying and never give in to the enemy.

Hannah prayed. Little girls fantasize about what they are going to be when they grow up. They will meet prince charming, fall in love, get married, have children, and live happily ever after. What happens when life does not unfold like she imagines? Does she blame herself or others? Well, in I Samuel Chapter 1 we see Hannah whose fantasy has turned into a nightmare. Does she stop dreaming because of the situation she's in? Of course not- Hannah became a prayer warrior. In the narrative, Hannah is married to Elkanah, but she is barren and desperately wants a son. Also, Peninnah (Elkanah's other wife) meddles Hannah because she was able to conceive. Hannah feels miserable year after year that she is unable to get pregnant. Hannah then goes to God in her bitterness, "And she was in bitterness of soul, and prayed to the Lord and wept in anguish. Then she made a vow and said, 'O Lord of hosts, if You will indeed look on the affliction of Your maidservant and remember me, and not forget Your maidservant, give your maidservant a male child, then I will give him to the Lord all the days of his life and no razor shall come upon his head'" (1:10-11). Hannah prayed so fervently that "only her lips moved and could not talk; only she spoke in her heart. Therefore, Eli thought she was drunk." (1:13). Hannah's prayers got God's attention and He answered her yes. "So it came to pass in the process of time that Hannah conceived and bore a son, and called his name Samuel, saying 'Because I have asked for him from the Lord'" (1 Samuel 1:20). Hannah was very sorrowful and prayed and wept greatly before the Lord. God saw her tears and her heart and did give her a son. Hannah kept her promise and gave him to the Lord for service at the temple and the child became a prophet. If you are a married woman and have not been able to conceive, pray to God and ask Him to bless you and your husband with a child. Prayer gets God to act positively on our behalf. If you continue reading to 2 Samuel, you will discover that God blessed Hannah with even more children.

Jesus prayed. Jesus Christ is the greatest gift given to mankind. Jesus was with the Father in the beginning and Jesus became flesh and lived among humanity over 2,000 years ago. Jesus Christ is God and is the King of kings and Lord of lords. Jesus Christ is our perfect example of perfect living and complete obedience to God. Also, Jesus is the expert on prayer. Jesus left heaven and came to earth to teach us the way. Jesus put off His Shekinah glory and wrapped Himself in man all to do God's will. Jesus knew how to pray, when to pray, why to pray, where to pray, and what to pray. In some of Jesus' human valley experiences, we find Jesus consistently praying. In John 11 when Lazarus died and before His crucifixion in Matthew 26, Jesus prays.

Jesus is all knowing and when His friend Lazarus became sick He knew that he would die. But God got the glory even in sickness and death because Jesus had the pow-

Chapter 7: Key 7: Pray

er to overcome sickness and raise the dead. John 11:41-42 gives us the prayer of Jesus at the grave of Lazarus:

> "And Jesus lifted up His eyes and said, 'Father, I thank You that You have heard Me, but because of the people who are standing by I said this, that they may believe that You sent Me.'"

As believers in Christ, we know that God raises dead things. He raises dead bodies, dead marriages, dead homes, dead finances, deadbeat dads/moms, and brings them back to life. If something is dead in your life, pray to God for a resurrection.

Jesus also prayed when He would have to die on the cross for us. Jesus knew no sin, but the sins of the whole world were about to be poured upon Him so that who so ever believed would be saved. Jesus Christ was the spotless Lamb of God and He was sacrificing His life for humanity past, present, and future. In Matthew 26, Jesus Christ is in the garden of Gethsemane with great sorrow and distress in His soul. "He went a little farther and fell on His face and prayed, saying 'O my Father, if it is possible, let this cup pass from Me; nevertheless not as I will but as You will'" (vs. 39). "He prayed the second time saying, 'O My Father if this cup cannot pass away from me unless I drink it, Your will be done' and he prayed the third time'" (vs. 42). At Jesus' lowest emotional time in His earthly ministry, He had enough wisdom to go to God in prayer. Jesus understood that He had to go through a painful death so man would be reconciled back to the Father and God would raise Him back from the dead on the third day. And "having been perfected, He became the author of eternal salvation to all who obey Him "(Hebrews 5:9). Jesus always prayed when He was experiencing distress, we too should pray when we experience painful situations. On the other side of the pain is the promise. On the other side of the storm, is the sunshine. On the other side of the cross, is the resurrection. Pray.

THE PRODUCTS OF PRAYER

The products of prayer are healing, help, and honorable living. In valley experiences, we need healing, help, and honorable living.

Healing. "Healing" means "to make complete or healthy or to cure of sickness." All healing and salvation come from God for Jeremiah 17:14 say, "Heal me, O Lord, and I shall be healed; Save Me and I shall be saved, for You are my praise." We must not forget to praise God before, during, and after a valley of sickness. Prayer is one of the ways to have healing manifest. God heals health, marriages, families, communities, minds, finances, heart disease, cancer, and any other areas you may need healing. James 5:13-14 states, "Is anyone among you suffering? Let him pray … Let him call for the elders of the church and let them pray over him anointing him with oil in the name of the Lord." As already mentioned, praying in faith produces the healing. If you pray and do not really believe God can do what you are asking, how can you expect to be healed?

Help. Help means to assist, support, or make comfortable. Jesus is our only protection and a very existing help in the time of suffering. If we pray to God, in a valley situation God will help. Psalm 46:5 says, "God is in the midst of

CHAPTER 7: KEY 7: PRAY

her, she shall not be moved; God shall help her, just at the break of dawn." God did not say that we would not have to cry or experience pain on earth, but He did promise that joy would come in the morning. No matter what problems we are going through, if we take the problems to God in prayer He is faithful to us when we call upon Him for help. God helps us because we are His children and He loves and wants the best for us. A valley experience is not a good place to be, but God can make all things better and new even in a valley experience. God gets the glory when believers believe Him and survive a valley experience. When we go through trials and tribulations in the world, understand that we are not alone. God is our helper and He holds us in the palm of His hand. In the midst of a valley, God provides when we pray to Him. Isaiah 41:18 says, "I will open rivers in desolate heights and fountains in the midst of valleys; I will make the wilderness a pool of water, and the dry lands springs of water." Help is available in any and every situation. Hebrews 4:16 says, "Let us therefore come boldly to the throne of grace that we may obtain mercy and find grace to help in time of need." Never think that a situation is too small or too big for God to care about. Even the hairs on our heads are important to God and God does heal incurable disease.

Honorable Living. Every Christian wants to live an honorable life. Morals are important to people because we all want to be treated fairly, honestly, and properly. We should treat others respectfully as well. Temptations will come because of sin and the flesh nature, but we can choose to respect God, others, and ourselves. We all need prayer. Hebrews 13:18 says, "Pray for us; for we are confident that we have a good conscience, in all things desiring to live honorably." We have to pray daily to live right and flee the temptation to sin. Our prayer lives need to be one to fight temptations. Jesus says, "Watch and pray, lest you enter into temptation. The spirit indeed is willing, but the flesh is weak" (Matthew 26:41). The works of the flesh are manifested in all types of uncleanness and immorality. Pray to God for the fruit of the Spirit which is according to Galatians 5:22-23 "love, joy, peace, longsuffering, kindness, goodness, faithfulness, gentleness, self-control. Against such there is no law." To live an honorable life in a valley experience, we must die to sin and live for Christ. Prayer is the key to unlocking the door to living a Christ filled life. Honorable practices include but are not limited to the following: God is first in our lives, loving our neighbors and enemies, telling the truth, having patience with friends and family, following policies and procedures at our jobs, nurturing our children, wives submitting to husbands, not stealing, sharing our resources with others, welcoming others, being faithful to our spouse, giving to the church, attending worship on a regular basis, and meditating on the word.

CHAPTER 8

KEY 8: SPEAK SUCCESS

"I shall not die, but live, and declare the works of the Lord."—Psalm 118:17

IN THE BEGINNING, WHEN GOD CREATED THE HEAVENS and the earth, He spoke it into existence. He said let there be and whatever God said came to be and it was good. "And the Lord God formed man of the dust of the ground, and breathed into his nostrils the breath of life; and man became a living being" (Genesis 2:7). God gave Adam dominion over all the creation. Adam was special because he was created in God's image and likeness. So, I conclude that if God spoke and it was good, what we speak can be the difference between failure and success. To survive a valley experience we must speak success.

THE POWER OF WORDS

The power of words is unique. Words create, live, and uplift. Think about it- words can heal, but they also can kill. We must be very careful about what comes forth from our mouths. Furthermore, we must be careful what comes out of our hearts and is planted in our hearts because Jesus says, "Brood of vipers! How can you, being evil, speak good things? For out of the abundance of the heart the mouth speaks" (Matthew 12:34). The tongue can be used for good or evil. Words that bless or words that curse can come from the same person. It's best to speak righteous, positive affirmations than negative speech or negative self-talk. If you have become accustomed to speaking negatively in a valley experience, you have to make a conscience effort to speak success. Speak to yourself that I am surviving this.

SPEAK LIFE

The words we speak have life. Proverbs 18:21 says, "Death and life are in the power of the tongue, and those who love it will eat its fruit." Words vindicate or convict. If you say "I can't make it." – You won't make it. If you say" I can make it!" – You will make it! Instead of talking yourself down, take the time to inventory some of the good things in your life. Speak life, speak prosperity, speak hope, speak faith, speak turn around, speak breakthrough, speak healing, speak peace, speak victory, and speak favor. Words can create an atmosphere for encouragement in the midst of life challenges. You will have what you say. Say, I am healed, I am delivered, I am set free, I am a survivor, I am a child of God, I am blessed, and I am loved. Proverbs 15:23 says, "A man has joy by the answer of his mouth, and a word spoken in due season, how good it is!" What you speak determines what you give birth to in a valley experience. To birth deliverance- speak freedom. To birth survival- speak life. To birth righteousness- speak truth. To birth successes- speak triumphs.

Chapter 8: Key 8: Speak Success

SPEAK GOD'S WORD

The language of blessings is God's Holy word. God words comfort you in the midst of the lowest valley experience. Psalm 119:103 says, "How sweet are Your words to my taste, sweeter than honey to my mouth." Read and hear God's word, do God's word, speak God's word and believe what you have spoken. Here are some of the scriptures to speak in a valley experience:

> Isaiah 40:31: "But those who wait on the Lord shall renew their strength; they shall mount up with wings like eagles, they shall run and not be weary, they shall walk and not faint."

> Psalm 91:16: "With long life I will satisfy him, and show him My salvation."

> Romans 1:16: "For I am not ashamed of the gospel of Christ, for it is the power of God to salvation for everyone who believes."

> I Peter 1:15: "But as He who called you is holy, you also be holy in all your conduct."

Satan will come to try to cause us to doubt the validity and reliability of God's word; however we must trust and believe that God is faithful and what He has spoken in His word is true and His word will come to pass. God is not a liar, and it is impossible for God to lie. Every blessing promised in God's Word, the Bible, are available to His children. We are guaranteed peace in the midst of a valley experience if we have Jesus. We are healed. We are saved. Speak peace in the middle of any trial or tribulation you face, knowing that you are an overcomer and more than conquerors in Christ Jesus. Satan is a liar. Sin does not control believers. 1 Corinthians 10:13 says, "No temptation has overtaken you except such is common to man; but God is faithful, who will not allow you to be tempted beyond what you are able, but with the temptation, will also make a way of escape, that you may be able to bear it."

DECLARE HEALING WORDS

Decree and declare healing words. Proverbs 15:2 says, "The tongue of the wise uses knowledge rightly, but the mouth of the fools pours forth foolishness." You cannot say everything you think or feel. The devil can put foolish thoughts in your mind and you must cast the evil thoughts down. Proverbs 15:4 says, "A wholesome tongue is a tree of life, but perverseness in it breaks the spirit." Words should be used to give God praise and worship. God hears our every conversation and wants us to put away filthy, dirty, unclean, vulgar, lewd, hateful, and hurtful language. Sometimes it is better to keep quiet, especially when you are upset of angry and want to use your tongue as a deadly weapon. Healing words are sweet to the listener and the speaker.

BENEFITS OF SPEAKING SUCCESS

The benefits of speaking success in a valley experience are innovation, revelation, and edification.

We have to prophesy to valley experiences. As we speak success, we get God ideas and His vision for our future. God sees believers as victorious and going through the valley on

Chapter 8: Key 8: Speak Success

the winning side. As we speak success, God reveals the way to get through day by day and God edifies us along the way. To edify means to build up or educate. Speaking success builds our faith and confidence in God, boosts our self-esteem, and teaches us self-worth. When we speak confidence in our God who is able, the strength comes.

Innovations. Innovations are new techniques, inventions, or concepts. When a company meets to discuss ideas and to brainstorm, innovations are produced. Advances in technology, computers, phones, communication and transportation come from God inspired people who spoke success despite many trials and errors. Speaking success brings innovations to believers. We speak success realizing a valley experience is not the final destination, it's only temporary and subject to change. Valley experiences may not change as rapidly as we want them to, but we can change our speech. Instead of lying, we can tell the truth. Instead of backbiting and gossiping, we can edify. Instead of cursing people out, we can speak blessings. A transformed life produces transformed conversation. Speak success.

Revelation. Revelation is the act of disclosing a significant truth. As we speak success, we announce what God is doing. Say, God is bringing me out alright and God is blessing me right now. As Jesus spoke in Mark 10:27, "With men it is impossible, but not with God; for with God all things are possible." We are saved and healed in Christ. We are overcomers and the victory is won by the blood of Jesus. 1 John 5:4 says, "For whatever is born of God overcomes the world. And this is the victory that has overcome the world-our faith." The greatest revelation is to know Jesus and the power of His resurrection. Then God reveals to us who we are in Jesus.

SPEAK TO...

We can speak to mountains, rocks, trees in the spiritual and the natural. Sometimes we need to speak to ourselves- if our pride is getting in the way of God working in our lives. In the hard places of a valley experience, we can speak to mountains and they will be moved; speak to rocks and they will yield water, and speak to trees and they will be uprooted. If you encounter a mountain of sickness, speak health and healing. If you face a mountain of debt, speak debt cancelation and prosperity. Jesus said to the disciples in Matthew 17:20 ... "if you have faith as a mustard seed you will say to this mountain, move from here to there and it will move and nothing will be impossible for you." If you have a rock of a hardened heart, speak and believe in the name of Jesus, and "out of your belly will flow rivers of living water" (John 7:38b). God told Moses in Numbers 20:8, "...speak to the rock before their eyes, and it will yield its water; thus you shall bring water for them out of the rock, and give drink to the congregation and their animals." Moses disobeyed; instead of speaking to the rock- he hit it twice. In spite of the disobedience, God still provided water for the children of Israel and their animals in the wilderness. Jesus Christ is our spiritual rock and His water is everlasting. God has an abundant supply of water in the spiritual and the natural. If you have unfruitful trees of bad habits, speak faith and the habits will be destroyed. Jesus says in Luke 17:6, "...If you have faith as a mustard seed, you can say to this mulberry tree, 'Be pulled up from the root and be planted in the sea', and it will obey you." If you

Chapter 8: Key 8: Speak Success

have a root of bitterness in your heart, pull it up and ask for forgiveness. Speak success to any valley experience.

Words have the power to create, but remember the ultimate Creator is God. God speaks, and a man lives. God speaks, and the dead are raised. God speaks, and demons have to flee. God speaks, and the winds, seas, storm, sun, moon, stars, snow, and rain obey. God speaks, and healing, deliverance, miracles, and blessings appear.

SPEECH PATTERNS

Speech patterns develop as we grow. First we cry, then babble, produce sounds, and then say words, more words, and finally speak whole sentences. As we grow in Christ we put away the baby talk and start talking like mature individuals. Paul explains the speech pattern best in 1 Corinthians 13:11, "When I was a child, I spoke as a child, I understood as a child; but when I became a man I put away the childish things." Instead of whining and complaining about the valley experience, understand that God is in control and speak praises to our God. Although things do not always occur like we want them to, mature believers give praise to God. Mature believers say, in spite of all the things we have been through, we are still blessed. The language of mature Christians in a valley experience expresses sincere gratitude to God who is bringing us out of a valley.

PROPHESY

In Ezekiel Chapter 37, God commands Ezekiel to prophesy to a valley of dry bones. The Spirit carried Him to the valley of dry bones and set him down in the midst of them. This narrative mirrors a valley experience. The bones in the valley were very dry as if the people were dead for a long time. He said to me, "Son of man, these bones are the whole house of Israel. They indeed say, 'our bones are dry, our hope is lost, and we ourselves are cut off' (37:11). Many times we feel hopeless and think that our life is over and we will never get better. Our feelings cannot blind us from speaking the truth. When we speak to dry circumstances, we do have hope in Christ, that our life is made brand new, and things do get better. God tells Ezekiel to prophesy to the bones. Ezekiel 37:4 says, "Again He said to me, 'Prophesy to these bones, and say to them, 'O dry bones, hear the word of the Lord.'" As Ezekiel obeyed and spoke, he heard the bones coming together (v. 7), flesh and skin coming upon the bones. "Prophesy to the breath, prophesy, son of man, and say to the breath, thus says the Lord God: Come from the four winds, O breath, and breathe on these slain, that they may live. So I prophesied as He commanded me, and breath came unto them, and they lived, and stood upon their feet, an exceedingly great army" (vs. 9-10). As God breathes on the situations of our life, we can live again. As God's Spirit enters our dry bones, we are revived and all hope is restored. We can stand because God is still God in a valley, giving us life in Jesus Christ. We speak success because Jesus says in John 11:26, "Whoever lives and believes in Me shall never die, do you believe this?" When God asks a man a question, He already knows the correct answer. God wants us to believe and speak what He has already spoken in His word. God knows the answers, and He cares about questions we may have. God placed Ezekiel in the valley so that he could prophesy to the dead things in the valley. Sometimes God will place you in contact or the presence of someone who is going through a valley so you can prophesy victory. When God allows a valley experience to happen, it works for your

CHAPTER 8: KEY 8: SPEAK SUCCESS

good and/or it could be for others. Sometimes you can be the only lifeline to speak to someone who is dying or has died in the valley. At first, God and Ezekiel were the only living beings in that particular valley. But when Ezekiel spoke as God had commanded him, everyone in the valley came alive. Spiritually speaking, you may be the only living (Christian) in your family, on your job, on your college campus, or in your neighborhood. God trusts you to speak life to others and help them live in Christ. Continue to speak life when all others are speaking death. Continue to speak breakthrough, when others are speaking breakdown. Continue to speak survival, when others are speaking failure. Continue to speak hope, when others are speaking hopelessness. Hope is a part of speaking success. Hope is similar to expectation and when believers speak success, we anticipate good things happening. Pray, speak success, have hope, have faith, believe God, leave doubt on the altar, go away praising God because it's already done. Hopelessness says, "What is the point of speaking about something 'I' can't change?" Hopeful people pray and speak success and believe God to change the things they can't change and trust God's power when human resources are limited. Hebrews 6:18 says, "That by two immutable things, in which it is impossible for God to lie, we might have strong consolation, who have fled for refuge to lay hold of the hope set before us." Speak hope in Christ and abundant life in a valley experience. If you speak life, God makes life come forth. God knows spiritually dead people can be brought back to life and unsaved people can come to Christ. People are dying in sin all around us; we need to speak about a life that is only found in Christ Jesus. As we represent Christ in valley experiences, we proclaim that there is salvation in the gospel. We speak that marriage between a man and woman is honorable. We speak that Jesus breaks addictions. We speak that repentance is necessary and Jesus saves. We speak that God loves truth. We speak love to one another. We speak that Jesus heals. For example, two people can share a hospital room – one is a believer, the other is an atheist. The believer can talk about the goodness of Jesus and pray for the atheist and win him to Christ even when both are in a valley of physical sickness. God did not cause the sickness of either, but the believer is in a place to speak life and the former atheist is in a good place to receive life. Agree with God, and God heals and makes alive physically and spiritually.

JESUS HEALS SPEECH IMPEDIMENTS

Jesus meets a man with a speech impediment in Mark 7:33-37, "And He took him aside from the multitude and put His fingers in his ears, and he spat and touched his tongue. Then looking up to heaven, He sighed and said to him 'Ephphatha', that is, be opened. Immediately his ears were opened, and the impediment of his tongue was loosed, and he spoke plainly." This man received a touch from Jesus and his whole life was changed. If there is a hindrance in your life triggering you to speak negatively, please ask God to correct it.

SPIRITUAL SPEECH THERAPY

Going through a personal valley experience teaches us how to speak success in the middle of it. If we find ourselves speaking contrary to God's word, we need spiritual speech therapy. To reverse the curse we caused to come by our negative words, we need to speak blessings. Spiritual speech

Chapter 8: Key 8: Speak Success

therapy requires a hearing change, a heart change, and then a head change. As my sister says, "a valley experience without change is impossible."

HEARING CHANGE

In Mark 7:16 Jesus says, "If anyone has ears to hear, let him hear." Our hearing has a connection to our speech. For example, if you grew up in a Spanish household, you will speak Spanish. English, Chinese, Swahili, Italian, French and many other languages are heard around the globe. You naturally speak what you have heard with your natural ears. If you hear trash all the time, you will speak trash, likewise, if you hear Spiritual things you will speak spiritually. God is multi-lingual and He speaks spiritually to believers in whatever dialect they hear. 1 Corinthians 2:12-13 says, "Now we have received, not the spirit of the world, but the Spirit who is from God, that we might know the things that have been freely given to us by God. These things we also speak, not in words which man's wisdom teaches, but which the Holy Spirit teaches comparing spiritual things with spiritual." Therefore, change what you hear by listening to God's word and hear messages from ministers of the gospel.

HEART CHANGE

Also, we need a heart change to speak success. Proverbs 22:17 says, "Incline your ear and hear the words of the wise, and apply your heart to my knowledge; for it is a pleasant thing if you keep them within you; let them all be fixed upon your lips, so that your trust may be in the Lord; I have instructed you today, even you." Jesus Christ is the greatest heart fixer alive. Jesus changes a person's vile heart into a compassionate heart. John 6:63 says, "It is the Spirit who gives life; the flesh profits nothing. The words that I speak to you are Spirit, and they are life." Jesus changes a deceitful heart. Jesus coverts prostitutes into praise leaders, bad girls into believers, pimps into preachers, drug addicts into deacons, sinners into saints, fearful into faithful, liars into truth tellers, homosexuals into heterosexual homemakers, prideful into pastors, murderers into missionaries, brokenhearted into whole, demon –possessed into delivered, and whores into witnesses. Apostle Paul was a persecutor of the church and blasphemer, but when he meets Jesus on the Damascus road his heart changes and he becomes a great mouthpiece for the gospel. Mary Magdalene was a whore, but when she meets Jesus her heart changes and she becomes the first person to witness Jesus after the resurrection. When our hearts change, then, we begin to speak words of life.

HEAD CHANGE

Also, we need a head change to speak success. Our minds and thoughts should be on ways to give glory to God. When our mind is on Jesus, we live in peace, sleep in peace, and get up in peace. Worry not because of the wicked devices of the enemy because our minds stay on Jesus. Trust in God that He brings you out of the valley and speak success. Isaiah 55:7 says, "Let the wicked forsake his way, and the unrighteous man his thoughts, let him return to the Lord, and He will have mercy on him; and to our God, for He will abundantly pardon." A head-change means that we have the mind of Christ. Jesus never said anything damaging about God or Himself. Jesus did warn the religious leaders of that day that they were hindering people from believing in God by their own hypocrisy. Colossians 3:2

Chapter 8: Key 8: Speak Success

says, "Set your mind on the things above, not on things of the earth." Colossians 3:8 says, "But now you yourselves are to put off all these: anger, wrath, malice, blasphemy, filthy language out of your mouth." A renewed mind will impact your speech.

SPEAK SUCCESS

Speak success, life, and blessings in a valley experience. Let not evil or negative people speak into your life. Do not receive a negative report or thought. God has plans to prosper us and gives us good things because He loves us so much. Let our ears, hearts, and minds stay on Jesus. The Holy Spirit will control our tongues if we let Him. Trust and believe God no matter what situation you are going through. No matter what the doctor says, speak God heals. No matter what your flesh says, speaks God delivers. No matter what your body says, speak God renews my strength daily. No matter what the bank account says, speak God provides abundantly. No matter what Satan says, speak God saves. God has the final answer and He elevates and exalts believers out of a valley experience. Speak life to your body, family, marriage, finances, mind, emotions, and every person you communicate with.

10 Ways To Survive A Valley Experience

CHAPTER 9

KEY 9: LEARN TO LOVE

"For God so loved the world that He gave His only begotten Son, that whoever believes in Him should not perish but have eternal life."—John 3:16

LOVE. MANY GREAT POETS HAVE WRITTEN ABOUT IT. Many great songs have been sung about it. Many people have wanted to find it and experience it. Love is important for survival. The opposite of love is hate. Hate destroys, kills, steals, and tears down. Love builds, heals, gives, and supports. God is the greatest lover of all time, giving us Jesus Christ. "But God demonstrates His own love toward us, in that while we were still sinners, Christ died for us" (Romans 5:8).

In the lowest points of a valley experience, love helps us. Love is a lot of things and can do a lot of things. We are commanded to love and have characteristics of love in our lives at all times. Also, there are many types of love, but the common demonstrator of love is giving, sacrifice, and compassion. We should love God, ourselves, and others.

WHAT IS LOVE?

Love defined is a strong attachment, affection, and enjoyable connection with another. In marriage, it is a word of physical, family, mental, emotional, or sexual intimacy. Loving is caring about someone so much that you would go above and beyond to aid that person. Song of Solomon 8:7 says, "Many waters cannot quench love, nor can the floods drown it. If a man would give for love all the wealth of his house, it would be utterly despised." Money can't buy love. Love is priceless; and if we learn to love, we can make it through any valley experience. Love is more than a feeling, it is an eternal lifestyle. When problems surround us and we seem to be in despair- we still love. When valleys are low and trials are tough- we love. When money is lacking and bills are due- we love. Romans 8:35 says, "Who shall separate us from the love of Christ? Shall tribulation, or distress, or persecution, or famine, or nakedness, or peril or sword? Satan and physical death cannot separate believers from the love of God. Romans 8:37 says, "Yet in all things we are more than conquerors through Him who loved us." Love is a powerful force that motivates us to endure any valley experience.

ABC'S OF LOVE

There are many qualities of love that I call the ABC's of love. Love is amazing, beautiful, caring, devoted, eternal, faithful, genuine, heartfelt, inseparable, joyful, kind, longsuffering, merciful, necessary, outstanding, pure, quickening, real, sincere, trustworthy, unfailing, valuable, wonderful, extraordinary, yearning, and zealous. Love is what everyone needs. Romans 5:5 says, "Now hope does not disappoint

Chapter 9: Key 9: Learn To Love

because the love of God has been poured out in our hearts by the Holy Spirit who was given to us." We cannot love without God in us showing us how to love.

HOW TO LOVE

We love universally, unconditionally, and unselfishly. God loves the entire world - saved and unsaved. Likewise, we should love everyone regardless of race, color, gender, background, or creed. If people loved universal there would be no more war, murders, shootings, thefts, and injustices in our towns, cities, states, and countries. A love for humankind will destroy Satan's plan to destroy America and global nations. We have to love and forgive each other and move forward to peaceful relationships. We all make mistakes and Christ has paid the price for our sins. James 4:2 says, "You lust and do not have. You murder and covet and cannot obtain. You fight and war. Yet you do not have because you do not ask." Instead of hating and fighting among our brothers and sisters, we should love, pray, and ask God to bring peace and His love to a troubled mind. Universal love is the answer.

Roman 12:9 says, "Let love be without hypocrisy. Abhor what is evil, cling to what is good." We are to hate evil, but not hate the person. We love sinners but hate the sin. We love people unconditionally. Unconditionally means without conditions or no strings attached. We do not stop loving based upon what someone does or does not do to us. We love even if people turn against us or walk away from us when we are in need of a friend. Jesus demonstrated unconditional love on the cross when He forgave sins. Jesus understood that His sacrificial death makes possible for whosoever that believes in Him to have eternal life. Jesus did not come to condemn people; He loves unconditionally and wants all to be saved. We do not have to qualify for God's love. God loves us no matter what we have done or did not do. God wants us to love like Jesus. Once again, Jesus loves sinners- not the sin. Sin separates humans from seeking out God's love because sin makes people feel guilty and unlovely. Unconditional love is what God has for everyone and He wants everyone to receive and give love likewise.

We love unselfishly. Matthew 25:35-36 says, "For I was hungry and you gave Me food, I was thirsty and you gave Me drink; I was a stranger and you took Me in, I was naked and you clothed me, I was sick and you visited Me, I was in prison and you came to Me." We show unselfish love when we give our food, finances, time, encouragement, help, money, water and clothes to the least of these. People all over the world are dying of starvation physically and spiritually. Homeless people need a helping hand of love, prisoners need a testimony of the love of Christ, poor people need nourishing meals and clean drinking water, and sick people need a visitor who will pray for them. It is love that ministers, prays, donates money, supply wells, and gives Bibles to others. Even when we are in need, someone will help us. It's not about your needs and it's not about my needs. Love is all about Jesus and His kingdom and when we bless others we are blessing Jesus. If you are in a valley and think it's all up to you to survive and no one is capable of helping you, then you are wrong. God is love and has commanded and compelled believers to love like Him – unselfishly.

WHO TO LOVE

Chapter 9: Key 9: Learn To Love

We can choose to love, but we cannot love whom we choose. In other words, we cannot pick people to love and hate others. So, who to love? We love God, ourselves, and others. We love God because He first loved us. Deuteronomy 6:5 says, "You shall love the Lord your God with all your heart, with all your soul, and with all your strength." We show God love by obeying Him. Jesus says in John 14:15, "If you love Me, keep My commandments." If we love God we will follow what the Bible says and love God more than anyone or anything in this world. God has called us to love His will, His purpose, His people, His plan, His paths, and His salvation. Love God because He is good, loving, merciful, the source of life, worthy, powerful, and mighty.

We also need to love ourselves and others. Leviticus 19:18 says, "You shall love your neighbor as yourself." You already love yourself, but God is your first love. When you love yourself, you want the best for yourself and do not want to harm yourself. Suicide is not an option even in a valley experience. Love yourself enough to come to Jesus, seek His love, and seek His provision. Jesus is always willing to help anyone. 1 Corinthians 16:14 says, "Let all that you do be done with love." If you love yourself, start eating right, start speaking success, start loving others and stop smoking, fornicating, lying, doing drugs, and other sinful activities. Women, it is okay to wear makeup, get your hair done, buy a new dress, etc. Men, it is okay to go to the gym or get a haircut, etc. It's alright also to love yourself enough to get out of abusive marriages and/or bad relationships. If a man or woman is beating you, he or she does not love you. Love yourself enough to deny yourself of hurtful things.

Love yourself enough to serve others. Jesus Christ

taught us to love others. He said to love Him, one another, neighbors, husband/wife, family, enemies, etc. How can you love others without loving God and yourself? Sometimes you will have to deny yourself for the sake of the cross. Loving yourself does not mean that you get everything or anything you want. Selfishness is to be absorbed by oneself. Love is not about me, myself, and I. Love is about him, them, they, her, and us. Jesus says, "If anyone desires to come after Me, let him deny himself, and take up his cross, and follow Me" (Matthew 16:24). We must give up the world's self-centered system and give into God's giving system. Titus 2:11-12 says, "For the grace of God that brings salvation has appeared to all men, teaching us that, denying ungodliness and worldly lusts we should live soberly, righteously and godly in the present age;" Because you love God, yourself, and others you will deny yourself of hurtful habits, fleeting fantasies, and adulterous affairs.

Jesus says in John 15:12, "This is My commandment, that you love one another, as I have loved you." God wants us to love: others, family, strangers, relatives, friends, co-workers, church members, brethren, unbelievers, husband/wife, children, and even our enemies. 1 John 3:16-17 says, "By this we know love, because He laid down His life for us. And we also ought to lay down our lives for the brethren. But whoever had this world's goods and sees his brother in need and shuts up his heart from him, how does the love of God abide in him?" We love others by assisting one another, offering services for free, giving to others, forgiving others, and sharing our resources. Jesus says even love your enemies. If someone hates you, still love them because God loves them too. We love our enemies, but we do not support evil behaviors. Forgive the person, let God

Chapter 9: Key 9: Learn To Love

handle the situation, and do not repay evil for evil. Romans 12:21 says, "Do not be overcome by evil, but overcome evil with good." The more people hate us and behave sinful toward us, the more we have to love them. The biggest enemy is Satan, evil spirits, demonic powers, devils, and fallen angels. Satan loves people to fight against one another and hate others. Satan is destroyed supernaturally with God's word, God's armor, God's love, Jesus' blood, faith in Christ, and our testimony. Love is the key.

WHY LOVE?

So, why love? We love because Jesus has commanded and compelled us to. Jesus loves us, and He commands us to love one another. A command is an order by a superior and is expected to be carried out. Jesus commands that we love and people know Christians by their love. Jesus says in John 14:24, "He who does not love Me does not keep My words, and the word which you hear is not Mine, but the Father's who sent Me." God loves, Jesus loves, Holy Spirit loves, and followers love. Even going through a valley experience, we love because Jesus is the authority in believer's lives. Jesus loved us enough to die for our sins and give up His life for His friends. We should also be willing to give up ourselves, our selfish agendas, and our egotistical desires to represent Love in the world. Love is commanded, and we obey by walking, talking, and living in love.

Jesus commands us to love purely, faithfully, and sincerely. 1 Timothy 1:5 says, "Now the purpose of the commandment is love from a pure heart, from a good conscience, and from sincere faith." We love God, ourselves, and others because our hearts are filled with God's love. Romans 13:10 says, "Love does no harm to a neighbor;

therefore love is the fulfillment of the law." We treat others the way we want to be treated, not the way that they treat us. We love with faith in God that God helps us to love. We want to love like Jesus. We love not expecting anything in return, but believing that God is glorified when we exhibit love.

Everyone can love. Not only are we commanded to love, but we also are compelled to love. To compel means to motivate, prompt, or appeal. A compelled love can be understood by ministers, missionaries, clergy, apostles, evangelists, humanitarians, etc. The love of Christ requires them to preach and serve when they may not be received well. With great sorrow, anguish, and tears they go into the world because God has compelled them to. Many have died on the front-line for the Lord but were prepared by God's love to lay down their lives to help someone else overcome a valley experience. As Paul states in 2 Corinthians 5:14-16, "For the love of Christ compels us, because we judge thus, that if One died for all, then all died; and He died for all, that those who live should live no longer for themselves, but for Him who died for them and rose again. Therefore, from now on, we regard no one according to the flesh. Even though we have known Christ according to the flesh, yet now we know Him thus no longer." Likewise, we can be compelled to love. No matter what trials we may have to face, bridges we may have to cross, or valleys we go through, Christ's love can shine brightly in us. The lives we live can be Christ-centered. Instead of being self- centered, love compels us to fight a good fight of faith, live for Christ, speak life, and pray for others.

TYPES OF LOVE

Chapter 9: Key 9: Learn To Love

There are many types of love: Brotherly, Eros, and Agape. Each love is different but shares a common theme, which is "sacrifice". "Sacrifice" means "to give up something in the interest of another."

Brotherly Love. Psalm 133:1 says, "Behold how good and how pleasant it is for brethren to dwell together in unity." When Christians come together in brotherly love they can change things in the world. Everyone is different and have varying opinions, thoughts, ideas, backgrounds, and strengths. When brothers and sisters sacrifice for one another and work together for a common goal- the team accomplishes much. If you are in a valley experience, love your brothers and offer each other a hand.

1 John 2:10-11 says, "He who loves his brother abides in light, and there is no cause for stumbling in him. But He who hates his brother is in darkness and walks in darkness, and does not know where he is going because darkness had blinded his eyes." Colossians 3:12-14 says, " Therefore as the elect of God, holy and beloved, put on tender mercies, kindness, humility, meekness, longsuffering; bearing with one another and forgiving one another; if anyone has a complaint against another; even as Christ forgave you, so you must also do. But above all things put on love, which is the bond of perfection." Brotherly love sacrifices time and energy.

Eros Love. Eros love is between a husband and wife. If you are in a valley of an unhappy marriage and are on the brink of divorce- you need love. You may have cheated or been cheated on and do not know how to forgive yourself or your spouse. You may feel unloved, under-appreciated, and just want some attention; however, do not give up on your marriage- there is hope in God. God creates marriage, loves marriage, and restores broken relationships. When a man and woman leave their father and mother and get married, they become one flesh. Jesus says, "And the two shall become one flesh, so then they are no longer two but one flesh. Therefore, what God has joined together let no man separate" (Mark 10:8). Proverbs 18:22 says, "He who finds a wife finds a good thing, and obtains favor from the Lord." Love in marriage is a good thing, and love in marriage is also about sacrifice. Marriage is for mature people and spouses must come on board with love in their hearts and minds. Husbands love and please their wives, and wives love and please their own husbands. The man is to treat the woman like a priceless jewel and the woman treats her husband like a respected partner and "submits unto him as unto the Lord" (Ephesians 5:22). Husbands and wives should also worship and pray together. God is the head of all heterosexual marriages, and teaches each person how to love, honor, respect, and submit. Ephesians 5:28-29 says, "So husbands ought to love their wives as their own bodies; he who loves his wife loves himself. For no one ever hated his own flesh, but nourishes and cherishes it, just as the Lord does the church." The Holy Spirit keeps marriages together, so we must always keep God first. A threefold cord between God, husband, and wife is not easily broken. Love and peace will be in your home. You will think about each other frequently and want to give the best to each other. Self-control, meekness, kindness and goodness will be in your speech and conduct toward others. Blessings will trickle down to your children and grandchildren when love is found in the family.

Chapter 9: Key 9: Learn To Love

Also, love forgives. In the book of Hosea, we see a man married to an unfaithful woman- Gomer. Although Hosea loves Gomer, she is a harlot and commits adultery. Eventually, Hosea gets his love back and says to her in Hosea 3:3, "You shall stay with me many days; you shall not play the harlot, nor shall you have a man- so, too will I be toward you." Hosea's story is parallel to many of ours. When married people go outside their marriage bed to fulfill a sexual desire they are committing adultery. When believers go outside God's perfect will to fulfill any want, we are committing spiritual adultery. Any needs we have God has already supplied them and any want we have God is willing to give it to us in His timing and He adds to it joy, love, peace, etc. We have committed spiritual adultery defiling ourselves with the things of this world. We may have idolized self, jobs, money, clothes, cars, good looks, sex, or other people. But God is a jealous God and nothing and no one comes before Him. We are married to God and if we continue in sin we are unfaithful; however, because God so loves He forgives us and gives us another chance. Hosea 14:4 says, "I will heal their backsliding, I will love them freely, for my anger has turned away from him." Sometimes you will get angry at yourself and others, but you still have to love. Often you want your spouse to "meet me half way". If your spouse won't budge, you choose to be unselfish enough to go and love them where they are at, and you meet them all the way. Love in marriage is all about giving up your will for the best interest of another person. That is what Jesus did for us- He went all the way to Calvary for us. We were all lost in trespasses and sins and were not even thinking about doing what is right. Nevertheless, Jesus gave up His heavenly glory and became a man on the earth, and gave His precious life for the sins of the world. What a sacrifice and what an example of ultimate sacrifice. What an eternal sacrifice and what an eternal Savior. Yes, and even in the lowest valley- Jesus loves you, comes and rescues you no matter how far you are.

Agape Love. The greatest love of all is agape love. Agape love is what God has for mankind. Agape love is full of grace and mercy being plentifully poured on believers everlasting. Agape love surpasses family, brotherly, and Eros love. It is supreme and perfect. You see, a mother may forget about her children- but God will never forget about us (His children). A man may divorce his wife, but Jesus will never divorce us (His bride). Brother may mistreat a brother, but God will never mistreat us. Jeremiah 31:3 says, "The Lord appeared of old to me, saying: 'Yes, I have loved you with an everlasting love; therefore with lovingkindness I have drawn you.'"

Grace causes God to give us blessings we do not deserve. Mercy causes us to avoid the punishment we do deserve. Without God's love manifested in Jesus Christ, all would be headed to hell at 1000 miles per hour. Jesus Christ is the only Savior and the only reason that God is gracious and merciful to believers. 1 John 4:9-10 says, "In this the love of God was manifested toward us, that God has sent His only begotten Son into the world, that we might live through Him. In this is love, not that we loved God, but that He loved us and sent His son to be the propitiation for our sins." We need to be thankful to God and live our lives in humble submission and obedience to the Father, Son, and Holy Spirit. Agape love is the love of God. We treat God badly, but God loves us. We may commit sins

CHAPTER 9: KEY 9: LEARN TO LOVE

and make bad choices, but God still loves us. God's love is perfected in us as we love others regardless of merit.

WHAT LOVE DOES

So, what does love do? Love is action and to love in action means that love: Covers, Gives, Transforms, Unites, and Begets.

Covering Love. To cover means to shield, to shelter, to wrap, to protect; to cloak, and to conceal. God covers us like a mother does her newborn baby or like a mother hen gathers her chicks under her wings. Love covers us in a valley experience by sheltering us from the storms of life. Proverbs 10:12 says, "Hatred stirs up strife, but love covers all sins." When we go around hating, talking about, and gossiping about others we are not being loving. 1 Peter 4:8 says, "And above all things have fervent love for one another, for love will cover a multitude of sins." Jesus has covered our sins by His blood. Because love has covered us we can also walk in love with one another. Psalm 32:1-2 says, "Blessed is he whose transgression is forgiven, whose sin is covered. Blessed is the man to whom the Lord does not impute iniquity and in whose spirit there is no deceit." God has forgiven all saints sin (past, present, and future) and sin is covered under the Blood of Jesus. Not only does the Lord forgive us, but He does not remind us of how filthy we were. Love is so deep that God does not bring our sins back up again. Psalm 103:12 says, "As far as the east is from the west, so far has He removed our transgressions from us." We have been pardoned by our heavenly Father and are now free in Jesus Christ. We also must pardon others and forgive our brothers, sisters, enemies, spouses, parents, neighbors, and friends. Saying I am sorry and please forgive me is the righteous action to take.

Giving Love. To give means to contribute, impart, or donate. God is a giver. He has given us many talents, resources, abilities, and gifts that help us survive a valley experience. The best gift God has given is Jesus who was wrapped in swaddling clothes, parented by Mary and Joseph, preached the gospel, healed the sick and raised the dead, and then was crucified on the cross. The gift did not end at the crucifixion; Jesus is raised and because He lives we can live also. The best gifts often do not come in big elaborate packages. Small gifts given from the heart of love are equally important. God is happy when people open their hearts and receive His Son. We are receivers of the divine power, grace, blessings, benefits, mercy, and the love of God. God open-handedly has given us everything we need in this life and in eternity to come. We receive what God has for us by believing on Jesus Christ and letting go of doubt and unbelief. We grasp onto the blessings of God and believe we have the things we ask for, as well as being thankful for the surprises God gives us that we did not ask for. God is glad when His children give from love. Love gives time, money, food, water, shoes, talents, offerings, presents, cards, hugs, kisses, thanks, godly advice, comfort, praise, etc. When you are going through a valley experience it is nice to receive a card, e-mail, phone call, post, or text message offering a word of encouragement.

God has also given us spiritual gifts to delight in. 1 Corinthians 12:28 says, "And God has appointed these in the church: first apostles, second prophets, third teachers, after that miracles, then gifts of healing, helps, administra-

Chapter 9: Key 9: Learn To Love

tions, varieties of tongues." Why would God give to the church if He did not love us? God has also given us pastors and leaders who love the flock and go to the lowest valley to feed the sheep and lambs. Jeremiah 3:15 says, "And I will give you shepherds according to My heart, who will feed you with knowledge and understanding." In a valley experience, it is a great blessing to hear and receive a powerful word coming from God through a pastor. Thank God for pastors who handle the congregation with love and care. Praise God for the Holy Spirit in believers who communicates to us the word and brings it back to our remembrance. Ephesians 4:11-12 says, "And He Himself gave some to be apostles, some prophets, some evangelists, and some pastors and teachers, for the equipping of the saints for the work of the ministry, for the edifying of the body of Christ." Love gives to all people, to the church, to the needy, to the hungry, to the broken, to the disabled, to the down-trodden. The work of the ministry is not a selfish work, we must reach out to the needs all around us and give love.

Transforming Love. To transform means to change the form of or convert. Love is a transformer. Love causes us to have joy, a new attitude, and a new nature. The reason we have joy in the midst of a valley experience is because "God has not given us a spirit of fear, but of power and of love and of a sound mind" (2 Timothy 1:7). Love transforms our fears and insecurities into boldness and confidence. Love transforms our lives from a lowly caterpillar mindset into a beautiful butterfly mindset flying above our circumstances. A butterfly may have gone through a low place (valley experience) but does not look or act like a caterpillar. Thank God believers who have been transformed into saints do not look, act, think, live, walk, or talk like sinners. When God has His way in our hearts, His Love transforms the chief of sinners into lovers. 1 John 4:18 says, "There is no fear in love, but perfect love casts out fear because fear involves torment. But he who fears has not been made perfect in love." Therefore, you may be going through a valley experience but God does not want you to be afraid. After your test, you will have a testimony. God loves you and His love surrounds and transforms you all the time. Believers do not need to have a pity party. Instead, believers should have a praise party.

Praise God because His love transforms you into a new creation. Jesus says in John 14:23: "If anyone loves Me, he will keep My word, and My Father will love him and We will come to him and make our home with him." If Jesus came physically to move into your house, how would things be different? Would you pray more, love more, read the Bible more, go to church more, praise more, and forgive more? Although Jesus is not here on earth physically, His Holy Spirit does abide in the hearts of believers and we are children of light. Our spirits are transformed by the Holy Spirit and we must walk in love, grace, mercy, and forgiveness. Jesus' sacrificial gift of love makes all things different.

Uniting Love. To unite means to come together as one body, goal, or mission. Love unites families, marriages, communities, and churches. Having a loving family assists you in surviving a valley experience. Families should be connected by both natural and spiritual blood. Mothers and fathers should love one another and love their children enough to train them up in the right way. Sons and daughters should love and respect their parents and obey the rules of the

Chapter 9: Key 9: Learn To Love

home. Ephesians 6:1 says, "Children obey your parents in the Lord, for this is right." Brothers and sisters should come together in love and not bicker and fight over the parents' attention. Parents should not play favorites- all your children are different, but should be loved equally. Families will be a lot healthier if love is in the household. Even in a blended family, the children should comply with the step parent. When families learn to love and unite they will live in peace and harmony. When the enemy comes in to divide the family, the family must draw nearer to God by worshiping together, praying with and for each other, and have Bible readings/study in the home.

Love also unites marriages. Ephesians 5:25-27 says, "Husbands, love your wives, just as Christ also loved the church and gave Himself for her, that He might sanctify and cleanse her with the washing of water by the word, that He might present her to Himself a glorious church, not having spot or wrinkle or any such thing, but that she should be holy and without blemish." Just as churches work with God, husbands and wives should work together and have no separate agenda. Marriage is honorable and spouses should be faithful to one another. Spouses should agree on Christian principles, financial matters, disciplining children, holy living, and sexual fidelity. There would be less divorce if married people learn to love, unite, and get on one accord with God. Amos asks a thought-provoking question: "Can two walk together unless they are agreed?" (Amos 3:3).

Love also unites communities. A community is a group of people living in the same region. Communities live together, work together, share resources, and make government decisions together. Ecclesiastes 4:9-10 says, "Two are better than one because they have a good reward for their labor. For if they fall, one will lift up his companion, but woe to him who is alone when he falls, for he has no one to help him up." For example, if a neighbor has gotten laid off their job, gotten ill, or suffered tragedy there should be some type of community resource to help him get back up. Community food banks, shelters, nonprofit organizations, churches, programs, and centers should be readily available in our communities.

    Love also unites churches. A church building is set apart for the worship of God and for prayer. Jesus established people as His church in the New Testament and it is built on love. The ideal church has many members, but it is one body. United by love for God and others, a church can impact the world and do amazing things. Selfish agendas and greedy church members cannot stand against Christians united in love. Hebrews 13:1 says, "Let brotherly love continue." Colossians 2:2 says, "...that their hearts may be encouraged, being knit together in love, and attaining to all riches of the full assurance of understanding, to the knowledge of the mystery of God, both of the Father and of Christ." We as a church body need to have a genuine desire to help and love one another. If someone is hurting, then we pray God to get them well. If someone is blessed, we rejoice together. Envy, jealousy, and divisions are like cancers to churches. Envy means you want what someone else has and are mad because he or she has it. Envy destroys the body and takes the focus off of worship to God. The same God who blesses your church member will also bless you too.

    We are thankful to God for all the gifts/talents/ blessings He gives to us and others. First and foremost, we

CHAPTER 9: KEY 9: LEARN TO LOVE

must remain loyal to Jesus and lean and depend on Him. Do not put your trust in things, talents, money, places, or people because idolatry and pride can arise in your life. We do not have to compete with one another for things because God owns it all and He freely gives blessings. Praise God for blessings, possessions, new cars, high paying jobs, big houses, mega churches, millions of dollars, musical talents, good singing, gifted people, anointed preachers and teachers, powerful prayer warriors, successes, good education, prosperous businesses, loving marriages, etc. We cannot view others and think they "don't deserve" the goodness of God because of their past, family background, race, gender, age, etc. Really, none of us are righteous without the blood of Jesus covering our sins and reconciling us back to God. Thus, the love of Jesus unites all believers into one body of Christ. Stop hating one another because of gifts and unite in love to minister to the downtrodden, unsaved, unloving, and sinful people. United believers can destroy the kingdom of darkness and fulfill the great commission of Jesus. Matthew 28:18-20 says, "And Jesus came and spoke to them saying, 'All authority has been given to Me in heaven and on earth. Go therefore and make disciples of all the nations, baptizing them in the name of the Father, and of the Son, and of the Holy Spirit teaching them to observe all things that I have commanded you; and lo, I am with you always, even to the end of the age. Amen.'" The great commission is productive if believers work together in love.

Begetting Love. To beget means to reproduce or yield. Love is a producer. Jesus is the Son of God's love. "God has delivered us from the power of darkness and conveyed us into the kingdom of the Son of His love, in whom we have redemption through His blood, the forgiveness of sins" (Colossians 1:13-14). God begat love and He is the first lover. In a valley experience, learn to love God, others, and yourself and produce fruit in a dry land. Love begets hope, love, strength, faith, and good works. 1 Peter 1:3 says, "Blessed be the God and father of our Lord Jesus Christ, who according to His abundant mercy has begotten us again to a living hope through the resurrection of Jesus Christ from the dead." When we think of love, we are hopeful to live another day and each day gets sweeter and sweeter. We expect God to give us strength and endurance that we may be able to survive any trial we may face or valley we go through. Since God has given us His love, we can show love and produce good works. Love produces love. As we love, we become more like the best lover –God. Jesus says in Revelation 2:19, "I know your works, love, service, faith, and your patience; and as for your works, the last are more than the first." We get God's undivided attention when we love and care for others and sacrifice our plans for others' needs. God sees our love and comes to our rescue. Sow a seed of love today, and see what crops us.

LOVE'S CHARACTERISTICS

What are the characteristics or signs of love? How do I know if someone loves me? The answer is found in 1 Corinthians 13:4-8: "Love suffers long and is kind, love does not envy; love does not parade itself, is not puffed up; does not behave rudely, does not seek its own, is not provoked, thinks no evil; does not rejoice in iniquity, but rejoices in the truth; bears all things, believes all things, endures all things. Love never fails...." Singles, dating, engaged, and/or married people will find these particular scriptures very

Chapter 9: Key 9: Learn To Love

helpful in their relationships.

GOD'S LOVE

"For God so loved the world that He gave His only begotten Son that whosoever believes in Him should not perish, but have everlasting life" (John 3:16). The love of God is perfect, pure, and powerful.

To be perfect means finished or complete. God's love is perfect because God has no flaws or imperfections. Psalm 18:30 says, "As for God, His way is perfect; the word of the Lord is proven; He is a shield to all who trust in Him." God loves humans and still love us when we mess up or do wrong. God still loves us when we experience aches and pains. God still loves us in a valley experience because no circumstance can snatch us from His hands. God loves for us to love likewise. 1 John 4:7 says, "Beloved, let us love one another, for love is of God and everyone who loves is born of God and knows God."

God's love is pure. Pure means clean, unmixed, and chaste. God loves the whole world and leaves no one out of salvation who believes in Jesus. 1 John 3:3 says, "And everyone who has this hope in Him purifies himself, just as He is pure." Because God's love is pure, Jesus' blood washes away the dirt and takes the stain away. The dirt is sin and the stain is guilt. Jesus was "manifested to take away our sins, and in Him there is no sin" (John 3:5). Jesus Christ is the spotless Lamb of God and we are made pure when we believe what God has already done by giving up Jesus. God's pure love enables us to survive a valley experience because Jesus washes us, makes us clean, prospers us, and presents us faultless in God's sight.

God's love is powerful. All powerful God draws sinners to a savior – Jesus. All powerful God heals and delivers and sets the captive free. All powerful God supplies our need, does what man deems impossible, and destroys the bondage of sin. All powerful God heals broken hearts, raises the dead, feeds the poor, turns the hearts of kings, casts out demons, heals sickness, and creates breakthroughs. All powerful God saves the believing world, walks on water, does miracles, and raised Jesus from the grave. Ephesians 1:19 says, "and what is the exceeding greatness of His power toward us who believe, according to the working of His mighty power which He worked in Christ when He raised him from the dead and seated Him at His right hand in the heavenly places." Ephesians 2:4-7 says, "But God who is rich in mercy, because of His great love with which He love us, even when we were dead in trespasses, made us alive together with Christ (by grace you have been saved) and raised us up together, and made us sit together in the heavenly places in Christ Jesus, that in the ages to come He might show the exceeding riches of His great grace and kindness toward us in Christ Jesus." Had it not been for God's love, grace, and mercy we would be left alone in the valley. Thankfully, we do not have to die in a valley experience, we are survivors. God is the God "who redeems your life from destruction, who crowns you with lovingkindness and tender mercies" (Psalm 103:4). God's love is so powerful that He frees believers from the valleys of this life. There is no shortage of God's love. God love is everlasting and will never run out.

GOD IS LOVE

God is love. 1 John 4:8 says, "He who does not love does not know God, for God is love." 1 John 4:16 says, "And we have known and believed the love that God has for us. God is love and he who abides in love abides in God and God in him." God's nature is love and no matter how far we try to run from God we cannot escape His love. God really loves us, but He hates sin. To know God is to know love and to know love is to understand God. God's love is like a loving father who guides His daughters and sons in the way of righteousness. God's love is like a mother who teaches her daughters to be women of virtue and holiness and her sons to be godly gentlemen. God is love, but He also corrects us when we do wrong. Jesus says in Revelation 3:19, "As many as I love, I rebuke and chasten. Therefore, be zealous and repent." Jesus does not chasten us in anger, but in love. Jesus loves us enough to stop and correct us and redirect us to Himself. When we go astray, we do feel the discipline of God not condemnation. God does not put diseases on us or punishes us with a valley experience. God allows us to go through the consequences of our own bad choices; however, God never leaves us in the mess, but is always there to get us out and welcomes us back with loving arms. To learn from our mistakes and repent is the wisest decision to make.

THE THINGS GOD HATES

To understand that God is love, we also need to know what things God hates. Proverbs 6:16-19 says, "The six things the Lord hates, Yes, seven are an abomination to Him: A proud look, A lying tongue, Hands that shed innocent blood, A heart that devises wicked plans, Feet that are swift in running to evil, A false witness who speaks lies, And one who sows discord among brethren."

Pride. God loves humility but hates pride. Pride means arrogance or an inflated view of oneself. Humility means modest, mild mannered, or gentleness. God exalts the humble, but the prideful are humbled. Satan was prideful and tried to overthrow God, but Satan was kicked out of heaven and will spend an eternity in the lake of fire. Jesus is humble and obeyed God and gave up His life for humankind and died on a cross. Now God has given Jesus a name higher than any other name and at the name of Jesus every knee shall bow and every tongue shall confess that "Jesus is Lord" (Philippians 2:8-11, paraphrased). 1 Peter 5:6-7 says, "Therefore humble yourselves under the mighty hand of God, that He may exalt you in due time, casting all your care upon Him, for He cares for you." We are humble when we totally submit to God and do not worry about what we are going through. Love, humbleness, and submission fit together, take the attention off self, and place our trust in God. Humble people also minister to the needs of others, but prideful people are self-absorbed. James 4:10 says, "Humble yourselves in the sight of the Lord, and He will lift you up." In the valley experience, humble yourself and God promises to lift you up.

Lying. God loves the truth but hates a lying tongue. God never lies and His truth is integrity. God loves us to tell the truth to our neighbors, friends, family, bosses, enemies, and government. Most of the lying comes from a selfish desire to preserve a false image we have created in our minds; however, if we want to be pleasing to our heavenly Father we must tell the truth to God, others, and ourselves. Lying, deceptions, fraud, embezzlement of funds, blackmail, stealing, and corruption are evil to God. Colossians 3:9

CHAPTER 9: KEY 9: LEARN TO LOVE

says, "Do not lie to one another since you have put off the old man with his deeds." Lying destroys churches, families, marriages, and even yourself. God helps us be truthful as we ask him for help. Pray – Lord, I do not want to keep on lying to You, others, and myself. God, please put in me your Holy Spirit. Your Holy Spirit will lead me and guide me in all truth. God, I hate lying and am sorry for the lies I have told. Please forgive me and have mercy on me. Give me the grace to become more like you each day. In Jesus' name, Amen. Daily, practice telling the truth. If you say you will do something do it, or if you cannot do something tell the truth about it. If someone asks you something and you do not want him or her to know your personal business – say I would rather not say or it is a private matter, instead of making up a lie. If you have committed a crime, admit the truth (plead guilty) and face potential jail time.

Murder. God loves pro- life, but hates hands that shed innocent blood. Abortion is a topic that many of us do not want to think about- but it is a reality. Mothers have killed millions of babies just because they did not want the responsibility of a baby. The baby is innocent and does not deserve a horrific death. So if you get pregnant out of wedlock, keep your baby or give the baby up for adoption rather than killing him or her. A baby is a life and he or she is not a mistake or accident, God purposely gave you the conception. In addition, people are murdering one another. Black on white, black on black, white on white and police on civilian killings are happening at an alarming rate. God is not pleased with the bloodshed in America because all lives matter to God. He is the giver of life. The Bible says you should not murder physically and even without guns, weapons, hands, or knives. How many times have we killed our neighbors, friends, relatives, children, and enemies with our destructive words? Jesus understood that words can hurt or can heal. Malicious words, gossiping, backbiting, and filthy language kills the hearer emotionally. Vengeance belongs to the Lord and He makes things right. If someone does harm to you do not try to pay them back. Instead, pray for you enemies and let God repair the person. Often, broken people try to heal another broken person, but that will not work because two wrongs do not make a right. Let us use our hands and tongues to uplift instead of tearing up. Let us use our hands and tongues to help, instead of hurting. Let us use our hands and tongues to praise and worship God, instead of fighting. The battle is not against flesh and blood, but it is against the devil in the spirit. Ephesians 6:11-12 says, "Put on the whole armor of God, that you may be able to stand against the wiles of the devil. For we do not wrestle against flesh and blood, but against principalities, against powers, against the rulers of the darkness of this age, against spiritual hosts of wickedness in the heavenly places." We should stop killing, warring, and fighting among ourselves. Love one another as God says - love. Put everything and everyone in the hands of Love.

Wicked hearts. God loves a pure heart, but hates a heart that devises wicked plans. A pure heart is a heart that surrenders to God. Pure hearted people desire good things and blessings for everyone.

Matthew 5:8 says, "Blessed are the pure in heart, for they shall see God." We must forsake all wickedness, immorality, fornications, adulteries, drunkenness, lying, homosexuality, idolatry, and evil communications. Reve-

CHAPTER 9: KEY 9: LEARN TO LOVE

lation 22:14-15 says, "Blessed are those who do His commandments, that they may have the right to the tree of life, and may enter through the gates into the city. But outside are dogs and sorcerers, and sexually immoral and murderers and idolaters and whoever loves and practices a lie." To come and live in God's presence we must have a new heart that is crying out to Jesus Christ because He gives new hearts. Ezekiel 11:19-20 says, "Then I will give them one heart, and I will put a new spirit within them, and take away the stony heart of their flesh, and give them a heart of flesh, that they may walk in My statutes and keep My judgments and do them; and they shall be My people and I will be their God." God loves hearts that do well such as worshiping, giving, serving, praising, sharing, loving, lending, praying, singing, teaching, admonishing, and believing on Christ. "And whatever you do in word and deed, do all in the name of the Lord Jesus, giving thanks to God the Father through Him" (Colossians 3:17). Going through a valley experience, do well and trust God to bring you through it all.

Running to evil. God loves feet that bring good tidings but hates feet that are swift in running to evil. Paul says in Ephesians 6:15, "having shod your feet with the preparation of the gospel of peace." Many people are quick to go to a club, bar, party, or casino. Often times these places are filled with immorality, drunkenness, drug abuse, and unrighteousness. We need to be more apt to go to the places where the word of God is being taught such as Sunday school, Bible study, and church. Feet are the body part upon which we stand or give movement such as walking, running, or dancing. We should walk into or run into loving places, not evil. What makes a person attracted to sinful situations? When we try to do good, evil is on every hand. The sin nature/flesh creeps in when we least expect it to. The remedy to the flesh is to walk after the Spirit and to run to God. Isaiah 52:7 says, "How beautiful upon the mountains are the feet of him who brings good news, who proclaims salvation, who says to Zion 'Your God reigns.'" You may be in a valley experience, and feel that your feet have slipped into running to evil, but there is still hope. Psalm 121:3 says, "He will not allow your foot to be moved. He who keeps you will not slumber: Behold, He who keeps Israel shall neither slumber nor sleep." In the darkest night, God is keeping you safe, preserving you, and holding you. Going through a valley experience, we need to go to places that will encourage us to praise the Lord and stand on His word. The things around us may be dark, but we are not dark. 1 Thessalonians 5:8 says, "But let us who are of the day, be sober, putting on the breastplate of faith and love, as a helmet the hope of salvation." Love and faith never disappoint. God loves us and wants us to enjoy our lives; however, if our fun is conflicting with God's nature it is evil in God's eyesight. God is the source of our joy and He wants our rest to be in Him and our relaxation and recreation to be with Him. If you are going to a place and participating in sinful acts, you are going in the wrong direction. God wants us to run and tell others about His love, His power, and His goodness. When we run away from God, we only hurt ourselves.

False witness. God loves a truthful messenger, but hates a false witness that speaks lies. False witnesses have caused innocent people to go to jail, men, and women to be murdered, and divorced. Who is the father of lies? Satan is the

Chapter 9: Key 9: Learn To Love

father or lies, but Jesus is the Faithful Witness. A witness is one who gives eyewitness proof, testimony, or evidence.

The devil makes false reports such as you will die, you are broke, you are ugly, you are a failure, no one loves you, etc. Never believe Satan- he is a liar. We believe the report of the Lord: we will live eternally; we are rich in Christ; we are fearfully and wonderfully made; we are beautiful; we are healed by the stripes of Jesus; we are successful in Jesus; Jesus loves me; etc. God is truth. God hates lying and bearing false witness and we cannot agree with Satan. God always rewards faithful and true witness. If lied on and you suffer persecutions for righteousness sake, you are blessed. Revelation 1:5-6 says, "And from Jesus Christ, the Faithful Witness, the firstborn from the dead, and the ruler over the kings of the earth. To Him who loved us and washed us from our sins in His own blood, and has made us kings and priests to His God and Father, to Him be glory and dominion forever and ever. Amen." Making false accusations and statements is of the evil one. Telling the truth is of the Holy One. Select God who loves us and do the things that are pleasing to God. When we tell one lie, we end up telling more lies to cover up the first lie. Our lies eventually catch up to us. We need to live virtuous lives with love, honesty, and sincerity. Learn to love the truth.

Sowing Discord. God loves peace and harmony but hates discord among brethren. In our generation, we call people who stir up conflict "messy" folks. Messy folks spread rumors, add and subtract details, and have people at war with each other. Messy people say, "girl I heard" and, "she said", "he said", but they are the people saying things that ruin the family, friendships, churches, and community peace.

10 Ways To Survive A Valley Experience

James warns us against messy people in James 3:16-18, "For where envy and self-seeking exist, confusion and every evil thing are there. But the wisdom that is from above is first pure, then peaceable, gentle, willing to yield, full of mercy and good fruits, without partiality and without hypocrisy. Now the fruit of righteousness is sown in peace by those who make peace." We know that God is not the author of confusion, but is full of love, forgiveness, longsuffering, and mercy. We will have peace with others when we mind our own business and stop sowing seeds of bitterness. We have peace with God by the blood of Jesus and He has given us the fruit of the Spirit. The "fruit of the Spirit is love, joy, peace, longsuffering, kindness, goodness, faithfulness, self-control. Against such there is no law" (Galatians 5:22-23). In the valley experience, we do not need someone kicking us when we are down, we need someone who will help us get up. We all need to be sowers of love, compassion, and courtesy. Plant seeds of love, peace, harmony, and reap the fruit of righteousness. 1 Peter 3:8-9 says, "Finally, all of you be of one mind having compassion for one another; love as brothers, be tenderhearted, be courteous; not returning evil for evil or reviling for reviling, but, on the contrary, blessing, knowing that you were called to this, that you may inherit a blessing." If you are sowing discord among brethren- Please Stop! Tearing someone else down will not make you better. If you play with fire, you may get burned. If you dig a ditch, you may fall in the ditch. If you dig in the trash, you may be stinking. Praying for others and helping our brothers strengthens all. God wants His children to avoid the things that harm them and put on His love, peace, patience, forgiveness, strength, joy, and salvation.

Chapter 10: Key 10: God First And Last

LEARN TO LOVE

God's love enables us to make it through any valley experience. God has already proven His love for us and we should love one another. We have a Father who cares and a Savior who died for us and rose again. We have God's protection, peace, presence, love, understanding, joy, blessings, and gifts. No matter what low places we go into, God comes and rescues us. Love is the force that joins us into the body of Christ. With Christ's Love in our hearts we are optimistic even in a valley experience. We pursue love and find it in God. Love is everything and God is Love. Learn to love God, others, and yourself.

10 Ways To Survive A Valley Experience

CHAPTER 10

KEY 10: GOD FIRST AND LAST

"I am the Alpha and the Omega, the Beginning and the End, the First and the Last."—Revelation 22:13

At the beginning of the book, I talked about putting God first in our lives and that is true. God is all that I want and all that I need and He will always be number 1 in my life, decisions, priorities, and salvation. When I read the book of Revelation (the last book of the Bible), I discovered a key that I had never realized before. God is last also. Yes, it is possible for God to be the First and the Last at the same time. God is everything, 1st, middle, last. Every moment we breathe is ordained by God, and every trial or valley we face is known by God, and God deserves us to come to Him at all times 1st, last, middle, always, beginning, and ending. By God being the First and the Last, are complete and have eternal life, victory, possibilities, protection, exits of pain, and entrances of His presence. We start with God and finish with God on our side.

BEING FIRST

In our society, everyone seems to want to be first. The first one to get something, the first one to reach a goal, the first person to walk on the moon, the first one to get picked for the team, the first one to lead the line, etc. First means coming at the beginning, the winning 1st place in a race, the valedictorian of a high school, or earn the highest rank in the university degree. Many want to be on the top and the head and no one wants to follow. Jesus warned His disciples of their upside down thinking. He said, "And indeed there are last who will be first, and there are first who will be last" (Luke 13:30). If anyone wants to be great in God's eyesight, he must be a servant of all. Jesus Christ came to earth to serve and give His life, not to be served. It is nothing wrong with being first, it is wrong to be first and not help anyone else achieve. Jesus advised the religious people who wanted to be first not to think highly of themselves. He said, "Woe to you Pharisees! For you love the best seats in the synagogues and greetings in the marketplaces" (Luke 11:43). Will you be a leader and still serve is a question that everyone needs to ask him or herself. If God does promote you to the CEO of a company, use your position to glorify God. If God places you as the leader of the praise team, use your position to glorify God. If you are a pastor of a church, use your position to serve others and glorify God.

BEING LAST

Being last often gets a negative connotation, because you think you are the loser. In God's eyes, all are equally significant to Him who come to His kingdom to serve. Matthew 23:22-12 says, "But who is greatest among you shall be your servant, and whoever exalts himself will be humbled

Chapter 10: Key 10: God First And Last

and he who humbles himself will be exalted." "Last" means "finishing after all others; ending; and final." God has the last say in a valley experience. God says we will make it through because He has already given us the ending. The ending will be better than the beginning. God was there in the beginning of a valley experience and is still there at the end. You have changed for the good. God carries you when you do not have the physical strength to endure. Isaiah 46:9-10 says, "'Remember the former things of old, For I am God and there is none like me, declaring the end from the beginning, and from ancient times things that are not yet done, saying my counsel shall stand, and I will do all my pleasure.'" God was/is God before the valley began, and will still be God after a valley experience comes to an end. God is First and Last.

ETERNAL LIFE

At the end of your natural life on earth, if you have accepted Jesus as Lord and Savior, you will receive eternal life. "Eternal means "everlasting; without end." This life we now live is temporary, which means it will only last for a short time. In this temporary life, we all go through valleys, face trials, and have sorrows; however, when we have eternal life, we will have no sorrow, no pain, no tears, no bills to pay, no lack, no terrorism, no war, no poverty, no sickness, no sleepless nights, no evil, no valleys, and no death. Revelation 21:4 describes eternal life with God: "And God will wipe away every tear from their eyes, there shall be no more death, nor sorrow, nor crying. There shall be no more pain, for the former things have passed away." Jesus is the First and the Last and gives overcomers a good inheritance. Nothing compares to the beauty of eternal life because believers will be in the presence of God forever. We receive blessings, celebration, wealth, love, peace, health, life, bliss, tranquility, and an eternal home with God. In eternal life, we serve God and reign forever and ever with Jesus. We reign and work in the eternal kingdom and possess good things for ever and ever, and will be clothed in white garments and receive a crown of life. James 1:12 says, "Blessed is the man who endures temptation; for when he has been approved, he will receive the crown of life which the Lord has promised to those who love Him." Our harmony lasts forever when we have finished this race and kept our faith in Jesus. Paul encourages believers in 2 Timothy 4:6-8: "For I am already being poured out as a drink offering, and the time of my departure is at hand, I have fought the good fight, I have finished the race, I have kept the faith, Finally, there is laid up for me the crown of righteousness, which the Lord, the righteous Judge will give me on that day, and not to me only, but also to all who loved His appearing." We are not trying to rush our time on the earth, but we understand that eternal life is far better than temporary life. All the good days we had on earth, will be magnified in Heaven. Jesus Christ's love is the reason that believers will have eternal life with Him. Jesus says in John 5:24, "Most assuredly, I say to you, he who hears My word and believes in Him who sent Me has everlasting life, and shall not come into judgment, but has passed from death into life." We are unworthy in our own strength to receive any crown- but because we believe in Jesus we have everlasting life. If you have suffered the loss of a loved one, comfort yourself with the promise that to be absent from the body is to be present with the Lord. Physical death is not final to a Christian, it's just moving to a better place. "For we know

CHAPTER 10: KEY 10: GOD FIRST AND LAST

that if our earthly house, this tent, is destroyed, we have a building from God, a house not made with hands, eternal in the heavens (2 Corinthians 5:1). Being with God forever is immeasurable. The opposite if eternal life is eternal separation. No one wants to hear God say "depart from me, ye worker of iniquity". But hell is a real place and Heaven is a real place.

A HEAVENLY CELEBRATION

The final destination is up to us, I choose Jesus and look forward to a time in which God will say "well done, thou good and faithful servant enter into the joy of the Lord". In heaven, I will rest from all trials and tribulations, and enjoy the presence of the Holy God in the company of fellow believers and angels. We will sing, shout for joy, and worship because our victory belongs to Jesus. We shall have a new name and eternal life forever. Heaven is like a gigantic celebration of our King of kings and Lord of lords. The Master of honor is Jesus Christ- the Lamb of God. We shall feast on His love, joy, goodness, righteousness, and grace. We will sing a new song and rejoice about how we made it through the valley experience. We will walk the streets of gold and take in the splendid view of Heaven. We will reunite with our loved ones who also accepted Jesus and never have to say goodbye. An eternal celebration is where we will drink from the fountain of the water of life and will drink in the Spirit a new wine. We won't grow old and "the last enemy which is death is destroyed" (1 Corinthians 15:26).

VICTORY

Jesus being First and Last through a valley experience also gives us victory. We believe that we have a heavenly home, but we also experience triumphs on the earth. We are victorious over depression, stress, and Satan. Depression comes when you feel hopeless, sad, and you are not quite yourself. Depression makes you feel utterly defeated, constantly agitated, and a black cloud overshadows your life and thought processes. Depression can come at a time where you may experience a sickness or loss in your life. When you are depressed you cannot eat, sleep, and go about your daily activities. You can also feel physical symptoms such as rapid heartbeat, panic attacks, shortness of breath, and anxiety. Depression is an enemy and you have power in Jesus' name to overcome depression. The antidote for depression is Jesus. Jesus says, "The Spirit of the Lord is upon Me, because He has anointed Me to preach the gospel to the poor; He has sent Me to heal the brokenhearted, to proclaim liberty to the captives, and recovery of sight to the blind, to set at liberty those who are oppressed; to proclaim the acceptable year of the Lord" (Luke 4:18-19). When depression tries to overwhelm your mind and body, start to praise and pray to God in Jesus' name. There is no need to stay in a prison of depression when Jesus Christ has already unlocked the door to freedom. Do not look to your circumstances, but look to Jesus and put your focus on Him. Jesus Christ makes you victorious over depression.

    Stress is pressure, worry, anxiety, and mental or physical tension. Stress is negative to the human body causing high blood pressure, stroke, disease, and cancers. Anger, alcohol, promiscuity, drugs, and excessive eating are ways people try to handle stress; however, to relieve stress, there is a better way. To have victory in a stressful situation, one must cast all his or her cares on Jesus. Jesus says, "Come to Me, all you who labor and are heavy laden and I will give

Chapter 10: Key 10: God First And Last

you rest. Take My yoke upon you and learn from me, for I am gentle and lowly in heart and you will find rest for your souls. For My yoke is easy and My burden is light" (Matthew 11:28-30). When the pressures of a valley experience seem to weigh you down, remember that Jesus is the answer. Jesus is the best doctor, caregiver, chiropractor, lawyer, marriage counselor, friend, mother, father, banker, firefighter, joy giver, peacemaker, sister, brother, police, teacher, coach, and Savior that you need. Trust in God first and last.

Also, we have victory over Satan. John 10:10 says, "The thief does not come except to steal and to kill, and to destroy. I have come that they may have life and that they may have it more abundantly." Satan is always walking around seeking whom he can devour; however, we have victory over Satan because of Jesus. Satan tries to destroy the saint's belief in God. Jesus defeated Satan, the devil, and demonic forces on the cross. The victory is won and we do not have to entertain Satan. Don't give the devil a place to reside and always resist his evil tricks. The devil has no power over you- unless you give him power. James 4: 7 says, "Therefore submit to God. Resist the devil and he will flee from you." Satan's fate has already been sealed by God and he is a conquered foe. Satan will receive eternal damnation. Revelation 20:10 says, "The devil, who deceived them, was cast into the lake of fire and brimstone where the beast and false prophet are, and they will be tormented day and night forever and ever." On the other hand, believers will have eternal blessings. Revelation 21:7 says, "He who overcomes shall inherit all things, and I will be his God and he shall be My son." We do not have to worry about Satan in this life or in the life to come- we have the victory in Jesus. Yes and Amen.

IT IS FINISHED!

Jesus being First and Last also gives us a finish. Finish means a manner of conclusion, completing, or accomplishment. God's salvation plan was completed on earth when Jesus Christ died on Calvary. For this cause, Jesus came to earth because without the shedding of blood, there is no remission of our sins. In the beginning of creation, when Adam disobeyed God a curse came into the earth and Jesus came as the spotless sacrifice to reconcile man back to God. "So when Jesus has received the sour wine, He said 'It is finished!" and bowing His head, He gave up His Spirit (John 19:30). Because Jesus finished the work, we can be finished also. Jesus finish is a complete finish, complete fulfillment, and a complete sacrifice.

A complete finish means that Jesus did not leave us out. Jesus said, "Greater love has no one than this than to lay down one's life for his friends" (John 15:13). Jesus proved His complete love for God and humanity by laying down His life and being resurrected three days later having power over death, the grave, and hell.

Also, Jesus' finish was a complete fulfillment. Jesus fulfills His promises. Jesus accomplished so much for humanity; His redemptive blood gives salvation, sanctification, justification, righteousness, and makes us a new creation. God is well pleased with the life, ministry, death, burial, resurrection, ascension, and the soon second coming of Jesus Christ. "He indeed was foreordained before the foundation of the world but was manifested in these last times for you who through Him believe in God, who raised Him from the dead and gave Him glory, so that your faith and hope are in God" (1 Peter 1:20-21). You will survive a

CHAPTER 10: KEY 10: GOD FIRST AND LAST

valley experience. Put all your faith and hope in Jesus Christ who is the author and finisher of our faith. Hebrews 12:2 says, "looking unto Jesus the author and the finisher of our faith, who for the joy that was set before Him endured the cross, despising the shame, and has sat down at the right hand of the throne of God." Jesus obeyed and did everything the Father wanted Him to complete.

Also, Jesus saying, "It is finished!" and dying on the cross is a complete sacrifice. In the Old Testament, people would have to sacrifice animals as a sin and trespass offering to God. As previously mentioned animals had to be sacrificed over and over, but Jesus made it one time and done forever. Jesus sacrifices His precious blood as the perfect and complete sacrifice.

WHY DID GOD ACCEPT JESUS' SACRIFICE?

Jesus' blood was pure and not like any human or animal blood. Jesus' blood ransomed us and purchased us back from sin and Satan.

WHAT SACRIFICE CAN CHRISTIANS MAKE TO GOD?

A sacrifice of praise is what God wants from us and He wants us to love one another. "Therefore, by Him let us continually offer the sacrifice of praise to God, that is the fruit of our lips, giving thanks to His name. But do not forget to do good and to share, for with such sacrifices God is well pleased" (Hebrews 13:15-16).

HOW CAN JESUS HELP ME IN A VALLEY EXPERIENCE?

Going through the valley, remember that God has already

made the way for you to go through triumphantly. You are not alone and you will be blessed in the valley and coming out of the valley. "For in Him we live and move and have our being, as also some of your own poets have said, For we are also His offspring" (Acts 17: 28).

WHAT ARE WE FREE FROM?

"It is finished" gives us freedom from sin and the law - the power of death. "But now having been set free from sin, and having become slaves of God, you have your fruit to holiness and the end, everlasting life. For the wages of sin is death, but the gift of God is eternal life in Christ Jesus our Lord" (Romans 6:22-23). We render ourselves as slaves to God and say that Jesus is our Master. We rely on Jesus completely for our provision, protection, and instruction. Relinquishing all our personal plans, we accept God's plan and will for our lives and we are controlled by the Holy Spirit and not our flesh. Sin does not dominate our thoughts and actions, and we live by God's grace.

GOD'S POSSIBILITIES

Because God is First and Last, we go from the impossible to the possible. Again, Mark 10:27 says, "But Jesus looked at them and said, 'With men it is impossible, but not with God, for with God all things are possible.'" God's possibilities ensure that things can be done and it will work out favorable for believers. Doctors may say your sickness is terminal, but God says I am your Healer. God makes it possible for old men and women to have children. God makes it possible for blind people to see. God makes it possible for deaf people to hear. God makes it possible for salvation. God makes it possible for us to survive valley

CHAPTER 10: KEY 10: GOD FIRST AND LAST

experiences. God is the Great I Am and there is nothing too hard for God to do. God says in Jeremiah 32:37, "Behold I am the Lord, the God of all flesh. Is there anything too hard for Me?" In the hard times, we look beyond our human strength and go to a higher power- God. In the good times, we still look beyond ourselves and see the amazing and awesome love of the living God. God makes possibilities out of all our impossible situations and circumstances. When you think it is impossible to survive a valley experience, believe that all things are possible with God.

GOD'S PROTECTION PLAN

Because God is First and Last we also get God's protection plan. If we purchase a large item such as a car, washer, dryer, stove, or refrigerator we have a warranty or extended protection plan. That means if something happens to that item within a set time frame we get a replacement at no added cost to us. These plans cannot prevent catastrophe, but gives buyers a little peace of mind. God's protection plan is better than our limited warranty or extended protection plans. God guarantees us His eternal protection and promises to never leave us or forsake us. His angel encamps all around us. Psalms 34:7 says, "The angel of the Lord encamps all around those who fear Him, and delivers them." With God's protection, we can walk through a valley experience without fear.

PROTECTION, PREVENTION, PRESERVATION

God's protection plan is all inclusive containing our protection physically, mentally, financial, sexually, family, emotional, social, and spiritual. God protects our spirit, soul, body, and mind. He prevented the diseases we could have gotten. He preserved our minds in the midst of the earthly departure of a parent, child, friend, or relative. He protected us from unwise relationships and deadly assassins waiting to destroy our reputations. In this world, we are surrounded by violence, pestilences, famine, war, wild animals, earthquakes, flood, natural disaster, and other events. All these things are occurring because we are in the beginning of sorrows that Jesus talked about in Matthew 24:8. But God has given us a promise of protection that says, "Now may the God of peace Himself sanctify you completely; and may your whole spirit, soul, and body be preserved blameless at the coming of our Lord Jesus Christ" (1 Thessalonians 5:23). Jesus also says, "But He that endures to the end shall be saved" (Matthew 24:13). God's protection plan protects, but also, He prevents and or preserves. If God does not stop the bad things from happening, He still keeps us from perishing in a valley experience. For example, a person may get into a car accident and the car is totaled, but the person comes out without a scratch. That is God's protection. Note: God does not cause bad accidents to happen- that is not His character. The devil is attacking, but God is still on the throne. A person may lose a job, but she/he gets a new business idea and better opportunities and higher pay on the next job. That is God's protection. The best preservation that God ever does is spiritual. Paul says to Timothy, "And the Lord will deliver me from every evil work and preserve me for His heavenly kingdom. To Him be glory for ever and ever. Amen" (2 Timothy 4:18). That is God's protection. So even in a valley experience of life, we still see God's protective plan. God protects us from dangers seen and unseen. God protects and prevents us from total ruin. Because of God's great wisdom, supernatural knowledge

Chapter 10: Key 10: God First And Last

and power, and love, He defends and protects His children.

GOD'S FINISH

Growing up, I always heard statements such as "He may not come when you want Him, but He'll be there right on time "and "Be patient with me, God is not through with me yet, when He is through with me I will come forth as pure gold". These statements always baffled me until I realized that God is always working things out on our behalf. Yes, when it seems God is silent He is doing His mysterious works. When God is finished, He makes all things new. We sometimes give God a deadline such as I should be _____ (married; richer; better; happier; successful; slimmer; etc.) by now. God's timing is not like our timelines. "But beloved, do not forget this one thing, that with the Lord one day is as a thousand years, and a thousand years, as one day "(2 Peter 3:8, paraphrased). In our microwave society, we want our desires and we want it yesterday. What if God is only saving the best for last? The best thing we can do is wait patiently.

God's finish is like a master carpenter/builder. His building plan is already in his mind and the blueprints are written and he knows what it will look like when it is complete. He starts with a solid foundation that is dug deep within the bedrock. He builds the frame and it does not look like much; afterwards, he adds the beams, wall, boards, and materials to the house. It takes time, but because he wants the house to stand, the carpenter meticulously saws, builds, cuts, measures, nails, fastens, drills, and completes the house. When the house is finished it is a beautiful display of the carpenter's handiwork. We are the house, and God is our carpenter. Jesus Christ is our solid foundation and we will live and not die in a valley experience. Jesus says, "Therefore, whoever hears these sayings of Mine, and does them, I will liken him to a wise man who built his house on the rock; and the rain descended, the flood came; and the winds blew and beat on that house; and it did not fall, for it was founded upon a rock" (Matthew 7:24-25). When God is finished, the product will stand. Although the flood, the storm, and a valley experience may come, you will survive.

God's finish is also like an experienced farmer. He plants the seeds, waters the ground, and the plant begins to grow. Only God can give life to a seed and God fertilizes the ground and waits for the harvest. The seeds that were sown in the right soil and in the right season were going to produce a harvest; however, Satan went in the field and planted some bad seeds and they start to grow beside the good seeds. God sees this and does not want to pull up the bad because then He will pull up the good before it is matured. God decides to let them both grow together until the harvest is complete. At the end, the reapers will separate the good from the bad and God will keep what He planted. Jesus says, " Let both grow together until the harvest, and at the time of the harvest, I will say to the reapers, 'First gather together the tares and bind them in bundles to burn them, but gather the wheat into my barn'" (Matthew 13:30). To be good seed, we must hear the word of God, understand the word, receive the word, believe in Jesus, then bear and produce fruit.

God planted Jesus as a seed in the ground and when He was resurrected He is the first-fruits of them that rise. Jesus says, "Most assuredly, I say to you, unless a grain of wheat falls into the ground and dies, it remains alone; but

CHAPTER 10: KEY 10: GOD FIRST AND LAST

if it dies, it produces much grain" (John 12:24). Although you may be in a valley experience, know that you have been planted by God. You are growing and maturing every day. God's word is also planted in your heart by faith. Produce fruits of love, joy, peace, longsuffering, kindness, goodness, faithfulness, gentleness, and self-control. God's grand finale happens when Jesus returns, the harvest is reaped, Satan is destroyed, souls are judged, and Jesus reigns forever in New Jerusalem. Revelation 21:6 says, "And He said to me, 'It is done.' I am the Alpha and the Omega, the beginning and the end. I will give of the fountain of the water of life freely to him who thirsts." No one knows the day or the hour when Jesus will return, but we know that He is coming back again. Just be ready- accept Jesus Christ in the free pardon of your sins and have eternal life.

THE LAST SAY

Three women of the Bible had God to seemingly appear last in their valley situation: the woman at the well, the woman with the issue of blood, and the woman caught in adultery. I'm sure these women tried all sorts of things to get well, but when they tried Jesus the miracle happened. One encounter with Jesus helped them to exit all their persecutions and pains and enter into the presence of an Almighty Savior.

A THIRSTY WOMAN

Jesus meets the woman at the well in John Chapter 4 and He asks her for a drink. Jesus was tired from his journey and sat by the well in a place called Samaria. Samaria was a city many Jews looked down upon because Samaritans were a mixed nation; however, Jesus looks beyond her nationality and gender and talks to her anyhow. This Samaritan woman was in need of living water only Jesus can give. Jesus says in verse 10 "If you knew the gift of God, and who it is who says to you, 'Give me a drink,' you would have asked Him and he would have given you living water." This woman was religious and Jesus wanted a relationship with her and with the entire world. The woman had five husbands and was living with a man that was not her husband. Now we see her persecution and pain. She was persecuted because she was a widow or divorcee. Either all or some of her husbands died or they divorced her. She was broken by relationships. This woman is very thirsty and human relationships could not quench her thirst. She probably was the talk of the city because she was involved in fornication with her new man because she did not want to marry again. The pain of death/divorce was too much to bear. Maybe she said within her mind, "I will just have a good time with him- no strings attached, no commitment, no feelings, no love, and no heartbreak". Thankfully, Jesus was there to show her a better way. If she wanted a good relationship, she should stop playing her games. Jesus said to her, "You worship what you do not know; we know what we worship for salvation is of the Jews. But the hour is coming and now is, when the true worshipers will worship the Father in spirit and truth; for the Father is seeking such to worship Him" (vs. 22-23) . Finally, it clicked in her mind and spirit that she was meeting the Messiah. The woman said to Jesus, "I know that Messiah is coming (who is called Christ). When He comes, He will tell us all things" (verses 25). Jesus reveals himself to her and gives her a fountain of life springing up in her and she goes her way, leaving the water pot behind, and testifying of her encounter with Christ. When Jesus entered the life of the woman at the well, she

CHAPTER 10: KEY 10: GOD FIRST AND LAST

got a new assignment. She was so excited that she could not keep the gift of salvation to herself. All the persecutions and pains exit the woman's spirit, soul, and body and God's holy presence enters the woman at the well.

How many ways are we thirsty in a valley experience? Our body is made of water and we need natural water to survive. Also, we need a spiritual drink which is only found in Jesus. Religious duties, rituals, and church routines cannot save- only Jesus saves. Jesus says, "Whoever eats My flesh and drinks My blood has eternal life, and I will raise Him up at the last day" (John 6:54). The blood Jesus shed on Calvary cross offers a new life to believers.

A WOMAN WITH AN ISSUE

Jesus meets the woman with the issue of blood in Mark Chapter 5:25-34. This woman needs Jesus to heal her physical body. The woman had suffered from a flow of blood for twelve years. She had gone to doctors and physicians but hadn't got any better - only worse. She was hurting, stinking, and ostracized from her family, friends, and community because of her condition. From the blood loss, she was weakening, feeble, and thin. She spent all her money on doctors, but they could not provide her a healing. Finally, when she heard about Jesus, she came behind Him in the crowd and touched His garment. She heard how He healed the sick, raised the dead, gave sight to the blind, and cast out demons. She said to herself, "God is not a respecter of persons. If he did it for them, He'll do it for me". When she got down low, and she "touched the border of His garment, immediately the fountain of her blood was dried up, and she felt in her body, that she was healed of the affliction" (Mark 5:29). Jesus perceived that power had gone out of

Him and looked to see who had done this thing. Then Jesus says to her in verse 34, "Daughter your faith has made you well. Go in peace and be healed of your affliction." Since Jesus came into the woman's life, her whole sickness was gone. Her pain and persecutions left, and she enters the presence of an Almighty Healer.

Going through a valley experience can cause us different issues. We may have issues of guilt, abuse, loss, pain, addictions, heartache, or sickness. Although believers face issues, God is with us, in us, for us, and equips us with faith, power, love, and a sound mind. No matter what issues we face, we overcome all of them in Jesus. No amount of issues or sin can scare Jesus away. Jesus is not afraid to confront and heal any affliction and forgive any sin. Physical, mental, spiritual, financial, sexual, emotional, educationally, family and social problems can be solved by Almighty God. Do not worry about how He works things out, just have faith and believe that all things work out for the good. A touch of faith always gets God's responsiveness. Just as the woman had faith, we all need to have faith that Jesus already makes us well.

THE CASE AGAINST A WOMAN

Jesus meets the woman caught in adultery in John Chapter 8:1-11. The woman is caught being unfaithful to her husband and religious leaders bring her to Jesus to handle her case. "The law of Moses commanded such to be stoned, but what do you say" (John 8:5)? Adultery is a sinful act and so is lying, stealing, fornication, homosexuality, cheating, gossiping, drunkenness, lewdness, etc. In God's eyes, all unrighteousness is sin. So, if the woman was to be stoned to death, how many more should be killed too? Where was

Chapter 10: Key 10: God First And Last

the man she was sleeping with? Where were other sinners? Jesus ignored the scribes and Pharisees and wrote on the ground, and then stood up and said to them, "He who is without sin among you, let him throw a stone at her first" (verse 7). Perhaps, someone had a stone in their hand but remembered that they had been a fornicator, adulterer, jealous, and then they dropped their stone; maybe they cursed someone out today and then threw their stone down; maybe they lusted after a married woman or man and felt convicted, and hence, dropped their stone; or they looked at pornography, and knew they had to throw their stone down. The Jews present realized that they had all committed sin and came short of the glory of God. Only Jesus was sinless and had the right to condemn the woman. "Then those who heard it being convicted by their conscience went out one by one, beginning with the oldest even to the last. And Jesus was left alone, and the woman standing in the midst"(verse 9). Then Jesus stood up and had compassion on the woman, saying to her, "Where are those accusers of yours? Has no one condemned you? She said, 'No one, Lord' And Jesus said to her, 'Neither do I condemn you, go and sin no more'" (verses 10-11). The woman called Jesus Lord, signifying that He had become her master. She deeply respected his kindness, mercy, love, forgiveness, and compassion, which He showed to her. We see Jesus showing up in this woman's case as a compassionate Savior, a loving Lord, a merciful Master, a forgiving Father, a kind King, and a gracious God. Additionally, thank God that His believers show love, and show mercy, compassion, forgiveness, kindness, and grace toward others. Because Jesus is the First and the Last, He pardoned the woman, although she was guilty of sin. To pardon means "to forgive or omit;

to pay the penalty for a crime." If the religious sect had their way, the woman would have been stoned to death, but thank God for His compassion, love, mercy, forgiveness, kindness, and grace. Also, we can see the accuser of the brethren (Satan) at work in this scenario. Every time we do wrong, Satan accuses us to God; however, Satan has been overruled by the blood of Jesus, who is our Advocate. The evidence is stacked up against us and we do deserve God's punishment, but Jesus stepped in and took our places. All of our sins can now be forgiven through Jesus and we can be free from the power of sin.

Our escape from the pain of sin, lust, adultery, perversion, unnatural affections, and fornication is the presence of the Sinless Savior, Jesus. "For He made Him who knew no sin to be sin for us, that we might become the righteousness of God in Him" (2 Corinthians 5:21). Jesus takes all of our sins and gives us all of His righteousness. First and foremost, we need to know that God is our Father and He loves us. No matter where we have been and what we have done, we still belong to Him. When we were little children and could not provide for ourselves, God clothed, fed, and protected us. When we were teenagers and started to develop into women and men, God still clothed, fed, and protected us. And now that we've matured into adulthood, many of us continue to sin against God; and yet, He still clothes, feeds, and protects us. God sent us His Son, Jesus, so that we can come back home safely. Sons and daughters, do not fear persecutions, do not fear hate, do not fear your accusers, do not fear naysayers, do not fear gossipers, and do not fear your valley experiences. God is our daddy, and we are His children. God always comes to where we are and changes our lives. God makes us brand new. Now you, too,

CHAPTER 10: KEY 10: GOD FIRST AND LAST

can go and sin no more. We can let others know that God is our Father and that there is nothing that He wouldn't do for us.

GOD FIRST AND LAST

Going through a valley experience with God First and Last, gives us an advantage over unbelievers. We overcome sickness, issues, sin, self- pity, death, and Satan. "No weapon formed against you will prosper and every tongue that rises up against you in judgment, you shall condemn. This is the heritage of the servants of the Lord. And their righteousness is from Me, says the Lord" (Isaiah 54:17). We have the hope of eternal life and a sense of completion in Jesus. God is not going to give up on us, so we should not give up on ourselves. God still heals, provides, protects, delivers, sets free, loves, and saves. To God be the Glory. He is the First and the Last.

10 Ways To Survive A Valley Experience

Chapter II

EXALTATION: HE BROUGHT ME OUT ALRIGHT

"Every valley shall be exalted and every mountain and hill brought low; the crooked places shall be made straight and the rough places smooth..."
—Isaiah 40:4

AFTER GOING THROUGH A VALLEY EXPERIENCE, THERE is one more step to take which is exaltation. We come out of the valley and enter into a brand new life. Because we went through the test with Jesus on our side, we have a good testimony. My testimony is I am (on my own) not perfect, but I serve a perfect God. I made errors, mistakes, and sinned, but God still had mercy on me. The things I did were not perfect. The things I said and thought were not perfect, but God forgave me and I love Him. I went through many losses, but God gave me back my peace, love, hope, sanity, and joy. I even love God, others, and myself more because of the lessons I learned in a valley. I gained a new perspective of life after the valley experience. My old thoughts were selfish, evil, and immoral, but my new thoughts are God- focused, sharing, giving, loving, good, and moral. God does not look at me and search for my past flaws and sins but looks into my future to see His plan manifested in my life. When the spotlight is on me, I do not get any credit. All the good I have accomplished in this life is because of a perfect God. God has no flaws, no faults, no imperfections and I am forever grateful to Jesus Christ for dying for my sins. If I inventory my life I have suffered loss, but I also have experienced great gains. I gained self-respect, salvation, love, joy, peace, and faith. The greatest gift I look forward to is eternal life with God. In the valley experience, I shed many tears, had sleepless nights, had heartaches, pains, and struggles. Nevertheless, through it all, I learned to be dependent on God- not depend on myself- not depend on a man- not depend on a job and – not depend on other people. I survived a valley experience and God brought me out full of grace and mercy. Because of Jesus, I am perfectly loved, righteous, forgiven, saved, redeemed, justified, and trusting in God. The hero in my life is Jesus Christ. My testimony may be different from your testimony, but everyone who God exalts out of a valley experience is grateful. We are exalted, have a testimony, seek God's will, make each day count, learn lessons, are alright, stop worrying, have an appetite for spiritual things, call on the name of Jesus, and leave a valley experience into the promise.

EXALTATION

To exalt means to promote, lift, elevate or rise. God exalts us out of the low valley and causes us to triumph. He exalted us out of sin, sickness, poverty, shame, low places,

CHAPTER 11: EXALTATION: HE BROUGHT ME OUT ALRIGHT

and low mindsets. We are delivered by God's will, and not by our own strength and will power. We are saved from a burning hell and eternal damnation because of God's love. God's will be done. Acts 13:17 says, "The God of this people Israel chose our fathers and exalted the people when they dwelt as strangers in the land of Egypt, and with an uplifted arm He brought them out of it." Some people may be comfortable in a valley experience and grumble or complain when they come out of it; however, if we agree with God and do not fight against Him and love, trust, honor, and obey Him we will be exalted and not want to go back to a valley experience. We are like strangers passing through this earth. We have a heavenly home and this life on earth is temporary. Because Jesus has brought us out a valley experience, we must live and die for Him. Paul says, "For to me, to live is Christ, and to die is gain" (Philippians 1:21). The things that needed to be killed are the things in our life that are opposite of God. God killed our sin nature, our lustful flesh, our old man, our disobedience, and our compromising with unrighteousness. Now we live for Him. We cannot go back to the way it used to be, we are changed into a new creature in Christ Jesus. "But now having been set free from sin, and having become slaves of God, you have your fruit to holiness, and the end everlasting life" (Romans 6:22). God has exalted us to a happy place that causes us to desire what God has in store for us in the present and future.

ONE DAY AT A TIME

We live this life one day at a time. Daily, we must trust God for our needs and pray that we do not yield to temptation and thank God He delivers us from the evil one. Jesus said,

10 Ways To Survive A Valley Experience

"Do not worry about tomorrow, for tomorrow will worry about its own things, sufficient for the day is its own trouble" (Matthew 6:34). So we must do our very best this day to live for Christ- tomorrow may be too late. No more making excuses. No more reservations. No more procrastination. No more postponing. Today is the day of salvation. We must forgive the people who wronged us and let it go. Today is the day that God has made and we will rejoice and be glad in it. We should not live a reckless and foolish life like the people of the world, but we can live wisely and enjoy what God gives us. Remember God makes and creates every day and He knows the past, present, and future at the same time. We make every day count by being thankful for our lives, using our gifts and talents to serve others, and always giving God praise and worship.

LESSONS LEARNED

For many of us, God brought us out of our valley experiences and taught us many lessons. God taught us lessons while we were in a valley, but did not put us in the valley to 'teach us a lesson'. We learned about love, prayer, praise, and life. The greatest love of all is God's love for us. God's love is unsearchable, powerful, and pure. Love casts out fear and we are free to love God, ourselves, and others. The love story is summed up in John 3:16: "For God so loved the world that He gave His only begotten Son, that whoever believes in Him should not perish but have everlasting life." God proved to us that because He is love and we love Him we can love others. We do not love by words only. Love is put in action by our giving, sharing, keeping God's commandments, helping our neighbors, and forgiving one another. The power of love has transformed us into better

Chapter 11: Exaltation: He Brought Me Out Alright

people. It's amazing that we love although we are hated. We smile when we are frowned at. We have joy when we go through trials. We have hope in the midst of troubled times.

We learned how to pray in a valley experience and still pray now that we are out of the valley. Prayers are our conversations with God spoken from the heart. And we are confident that when we pray, God will answer. When we pray to God sincerely, He speaks one word and changes a valley experience. For example, in the middle of the night, while you were asleep, you heard the solution to a problem you prayed about. You know it had to be the voice of God because you could not think of the answer on your own. We have prayed and seen results time and time again. Prayer is not only for us- it is for others also. Prayers of righteous men and women give God the opportunity to work on our behalf. So when we pray believing that God has the power to grant our requests we can ask anything in Jesus' name. No prayer = no power. Little prayer = little power. Much prayer = much power. "Men should always pray and not lose heart" (Luke 18:1). God never gets tired of our prayers and loves for His children to pray to Him anytime day or night. We pray in faith and believe that it's already done.

We learned to praise in the valley and still praise. Praise is our sacrifice to God. He deserves our worship and praise because He gave us breath. God is everything we need and God has everything we could imagine or think we want. We praise God for who He is, what He has done, and what He will do in our future. God is Omnipotent, Omnipresent, Omniscient, Sovereign and All-Knowing. He knows the intents of our hearts and the motives behind everything we have done; what we do, or will do in the next minute. We praise God because we love God and if He never gives us another blessing we still praise Him. He wakes us up every day, gives us the ability to think and function, and leads and guides us in all truth. We learn to praise God because He is our Savior, Provider, Comforter, Healer, Deliverer, Mighty God, King of Kings, and Lord of Lords. At all times, we praise the Lord. God gives us eternal life and has also given us Jesus and His Holy Spirit who empowers us to finish strong.

We learned about life going through and coming out of a valley experience alright. Our life is filled with highs and lows, trials and tests, setbacks and set-ups, and eventually breakthroughs. Because of the consequences of our sins, Satan's attacks, and human errors we have tribulations, but we still overcame the valley in Jesus. Jesus is bigger than our sins, Satan, and human error. We will remain exalted and we will keep looking up to Jesus. The pain we had did not and will not last forever. Life is about God and if we survive it is all about God. The exalted life is better than before. God remained faithful and verified that the latter house is greater than the former house. God is not afraid to come after you wherever you may be. Even in the dark places, you have to be willing to follow Him out. And when He brings you out you will not forget the lessons you learned.

I AM ALRIGHT

In spite of every valley I went through, I am alright. I came out of a valley okay, fine, transformed, pleasing to God, worthy, and sane. I survived and made it out alive. 2 Corinthians 4:8-10 says it best, "We are hard-pressed on ev-

CHAPTER 11: EXALTATION: HE BROUGHT ME OUT ALRIGHT

ery side, yet not crushed; we are perplexed, but not in despair; persecuted, but not forsaken; struck down, but not destroyed- always carrying about in the body the dying of the Lord Jesus, that the life of Jesus also may be manifested in our body." We are survivors physically, mentally, emotionally, sexually, family/socially, financially, and spiritually. What tried to kill us and kill our spirit did not defeat us because we have Jesus on our side. When the pressures of life had us down, we could have lost our minds and stopped living; however, God gave us the strength to endure the valleys of trials, tests, hardships, struggles, storms, and discouragements. God's power, protection, love, presence, provision, word, grace, mercy, and wisdom brought us out all right. When our money ran out, family members were ill, and we had pain in our body we never lost faith. God brought us through and now has set us in high places that are smooth and straight. Proverbs 3:5-6 says, "Trust in the Lord with all your heart, and lean not on your own understanding; in all your ways acknowledge Him, and He shall direct your paths."

STOP WORRYING

I had problems and went through a valley experience, but I don't have any worries. Famous "worldly" people think they don't have any worries because they have achieved a social status and large fan base. In the physical sense, celebrities have lots of money, fans, cars, houses, women or men, material possessions, and affluence. In the spiritual sense, some celebrities may be broke and in need of true prosperity only found in Jesus Christ. I don't have any worries because God is in control of my life. I don't worry about what I don't have because God has everything. I do not worry about the wicked, because God says in Psalm 37:1-2, "Do not fret because of evildoers, nor be envious of the workers of iniquity, for they shall soon be cut down like grass and wither as the green herb." I don't worry about money because all the silver and gold belongs to my Father. I don't worry about difficulties because I cast my cares upon Jesus. I don't worry about tomorrow because God takes care of my daily needs. I don't worry about my salvation because I believe Jesus died for me. I don't worry about earthly recognition because God gets all the glory. I don't worry about sickness because Jesus has healed me. I don't worry about my lifespan because I live for eternity. So, I don't worry about anything because God has taken care of everything. In everything, I come to the conclusion to stop worrying and love God more than anyone or anything.

A SPIRITUAL APPETITE

Since being exalted from a low place, we have an appetite for spiritual things. We desire to feed on God's word and His faithfulness. Jesus Christ is living bread and if we feast on Him we shall never die. A good appetite is an indication that you are well because sick people do not have a desire to eat. God's word is strength for our bodies, food for our souls, and nourishment to our spirits. Just as our natural bodies need healthy food and drink, so does our souls and spirits. We are satisfied and full of life and hope when we feast on Jesus. Jesus says, "This is the bread which came down from heaven—not as your fathers ate the manna, and are dead. He who eats this bread will live forever" (John 6:58). If we continue to feed our flesh with junk food we will be unhealthy. Likewise, if we continue to feed our spirits with junk we will be unhealthy. A healthy spirit desires

CHAPTER 11: EXALTATION: HE BROUGHT ME OUT ALRIGHT

the genuine word of God. We feed our spirits by believing Jesus, walking in love, reading the Bible, going to church, worshiping God, praying for one another, and learning sound spiritual doctrine. Starve out fear, doubt, hate, unbelief, pride, heresies, lust, gossip, lying, evil communication, discord, and every sin. As our appetites for spiritual things increase, we no longer crave the ungodly things. Temptations to indulge the flesh will come, so we must continually put our faith in God. James 4:7-8 says, "Submit yourself to God, resist the devil, and he will flee from you. Draw near to God and He will draw near to you. Cleanse your hands, you sinners, and purify your hearts, you double-minded." Eating spiritual food is allowing God's word to take root in our ears, hearts, minds, thoughts, souls, and spirits.

CALL ON THE NAME OF JESUS

God saved us and exalted us out of a valley experience because of His great love for us. We must forever call on the name of Jesus and thank Him for reconciling us back to God. What's in a name? Before the baby is born, parents try to decide what their child's name will be. Will the child be Michael, Maria, John, Sue, or Madison? In former times, names meant something and the child would take on the characteristics of his/her name. For example, Judah meant "praise", Moses meant "drawn out the water", Samuel meant "heard of God", and Peter meant "rock". No matter what name has been given in the earth or in heaven there is no other name more powerful than the name of Jesus. Isaiah prophesied of his name declaring, "For unto us a child is born, unto us a Son is given; and the government will be upon His shoulder. And His name will be called Wonderful, Counselor, Mighty God, Everlasting Father, Prince of Peace" (Isaiah 9:6). The angel, Gabriel, appeared to the Virgin Mary and told her, "And behold, you will conceive in your womb and bring forth a Son, and shall call His name Jesus. He will be great, and will be called the Son of the Highest, and the Lord God will give Him the throne of His father David. And He will reign over the house of Jacob forever, and of His kingdom there will be no end" (Luke 1:31-33). The name Jesus means Savior or Immanuel which is interpreted "God with us". Therefore, if anyone believes and confesses the Lord Jesus they are saved. Romans 10:9 says, "That if you confess with your mouth the Lord Jesus and believe in your heart that God has raised Him from the dead, you will be saved." Jesus saves us from sickness, death, disease, hell, and from our sins. Jesus demonstrated His love for us by being a living example of holiness, humility, obedience, and even died on the cross for humanity and was raised again. Jesus says His name is I Am. He said, I am the bread of life; I am the light of the world; I am from above; I am the good shepherd; I am the door; I am the resurrection and the life; I am the way, the truth, and the life; I am the true vine, I am Alpha and Omega; The First and the Last; The Beginning and the End; which is, which was, and which is to come, the Almighty; I am He that liveth and was dead; I am alive forever more, I am the Root and Offspring of David and the Bright and Morning Star. There is no other name more worthy to be called on than the name of Jesus. Jesus is bread when we are hungry, water when we are thirsty, a friend to the friendless, a father to the fatherless, a company keeper, a trusted confidant and comforter, a savior, a rewarder, a loving Lord, and peace in a valley. Proverbs 18:10 says, "The name of the Lord is a strong tower; the righteous run to it and are safe." Acts 4:12

CHAPTER 11: EXALTATION: HE BROUGHT ME OUT ALRIGHT

says, "Nor is there salvation in any other, for there is no other name under heaven given among men by which we must be saved." Muhammad cannot save, Buddha cannot save, Satan cannot save, Baal cannot save, Jezebel cannot save, Confucius cannot save, and idols cannot save. Because Jesus saves, the weak can say "I am strong", the poor can say, "I am rich", the bound can say "I am delivered", and the sick can say "I am healed". Thank God for the name of Jesus and because of it lost people can be found. We once were in a valley experience, but now we are exalted.

A PLAN FOR EXALTATION

Before we went into the valley, God already had an exit strategy in place. His plan was not based upon what we could do to fix the situation. His plan of exaltation was based upon His divine power, purpose, plan, and promises. Nothing happened to us that God did not allow or permit. God helped us to go through a valley and we came out still praising Him. All things worked out for our good, even the situations the devil thought would kill us. God brought us out of valley experiences into His promise. Now we are standing on divine power, designed plans, desired purposes, and divine promises.

DIVINE POWER

God's divine power kept us in a valley experience and keeps us now that we have been exalted into the Promised Land. All power belongs to God, Jesus, and the Holy Spirit. God is our creator, sustainer, power source, and uplifts us out with His hand. 1 Peter 1:3 says, "As His divine power has given to us all things that pertain to life and godliness, through the knowledge of Him who called us by glory and virtue." We faced problems both of external and internal origins. We faced attacks from outside forces as well as from inside our own minds. But, because God's power is unlimited, He rescued us from the enemy without and the enemy within ourselves. Every stronghold has been broken by the power of the blood of Jesus Christ. We are now free to walk in love, peace, holiness, joy, and safety. God is on our side and we do not have to fear. We are walking in victory and divine power. The authority we have in the name of Jesus is why we speak to valleys, sickness, mountains, poverty, and devils.

DESIGNED PLANS

God's plan is specific for individuals. My plan is not your plan and your plan is not my plan. Everyone is different, but God sees potential in everyone. My valley experience was different from your valley experience, but we both experienced the same result- exaltation. God is our designer and manager. God can make something out of nothing. God calls those things that be not as though they are and it must become what God speaks. God plans the end of a thing from the beginning. God clothes the naked, heals the sick, and feeds the hungry. God uses people to prophesy His words, preach the gospel, and work miracles by His Name. If we follow God's plan and have faith to believe we can do the impossible. "For it is God who works in you both to will and to do for His good pleasure" (Philippians 2:13). So, whatever plan God has designed for us we can accomplish it by His strength. God has called us out of darkness into His marvelous light and we can shine brightly in a dark and cold generation. God has given us hidden talents, gifts, and abilities and we never realized them until we

CHAPTER 11: EXALTATION: HE BROUGHT ME OUT ALRIGHT

went through a low place. God always knows what talents, gifts, abilities are inside us because He placed them in us by His designed plans. The valley experience uncovered the hidden things and we learned that we could not bear good fruit until we live in Christ's love.

DESIRED PURPOSES

God's desired purpose is that no one should be lost. Therefore, if God saved us out of a valley experience, He can get anyone out. Now that we are out and exalted above the valley, and we see friends, family members, and even our enemies still going through a low place we need to tell them about how we made it out alive (Jesus is the way). People can learn about God from the life we live. Jesus came into the world to save us and He knew and fulfilled His purpose. John 12:32 says, "And I, if I am lifted up from the earth, I will draw all people to Myself." Believers should want to draw people to Christ, not drive them away from Christ. Also, our purpose is to worship and serve God in spirit and truth. Our past lives are gone and we live as new creations created in Christ for good works.

DIVINE PROMISES

God's divine promises are irrevocable. If God says it, then it will come to pass. God promises us the Holy Spirit, rest, Jesus' first and second coming, and many more assurances. God does not make promises and not fulfill them. The Holy Spirit came into believers on the day of Pentecost and is still in us. Acts 2:4 says, "And they were all filled with the Holy Spirit and began to speak with other tongues as the Spirit gave them utterance." The Holy Spirit was with God in the beginning and is still alive and well today and He helps us live a Christian life. The Holy Spirit is our Comforter, Helper, and Teacher. Jesus promised the disciples, "But the Helper, the Holy Spirit whom the Father will send in My name, He will teach you all things, and bring to your remembrance all thing that I said to you" (Luke 14:26). The Holy Spirit dwells in believers and is grieved when we disobey God's word. Peter talks about spiritual conduct and divine promises in 2 Peter 1:4-8:

> "By which have been given to us exceedingly great and precious promises, that through these you may be partakers of the divine nature, having escaped the corruption that is in the world through lust. But also, for this very reason, giving all diligence, add to your faith virtue, to virtue knowledge, to knowledge, self-control, to self-control perseverance, to perseverance godliness, to godliness brotherly kindness and to brotherly kindness love. For if these things are yours and abound, you will be neither barren nor unfruitful in the knowledge of our Lord Jesus Christ."

The Holy Spirit helps us live holy, faithful, and loving lives and convicts us when we do wrong. The Spirit teaches us that we are God's children and we are heirs to the promises of God and can be partakers of Jesus' divine nature and character.

God has also promised us rest and a soon returning of Jesus. Jesus is coming back again to reward the righteous and battle against the wicked. Revelation 16:15 says, "Behold I am coming as a thief, blessed is he who watches, and keeps his garments, lest he walk naked and they see his

CHAPTER 11: EXALTATION: HE BROUGHT ME OUT ALRIGHT

shame." The angels also testified that Jesus is coming back on a cloud in the sky someday. Luke writes in Acts 1:11, "Who also said, 'men of Galilee, why do you stand gazing up into heaven?' This same Jesus, who was taken up from you into heaven, will so come in like manner as you saw Him go into heaven.'" We are confident that Jesus will return as He has promised. We must continue to walk in faith and live exalted above a valley experience. "For yet a little while, and He who is coming will not tarry. Now the just shall live by faith; but if anyone draws back, my soul has no pleasure in him" (Hebrews 10:37-38).

WHO OR WHAT CAN SEPARATE US FROM THE LOVE OF GOD?

We have Jesus Christ saving and restoring our broken relationship with God. Now we have the opportunity and promise to live and rest with God forever. Not only did God choose us, but we also make Him our choice. Nothing and no-one can separate believers from the love of God which is found in Christ Jesus. Romans 8:38-39 says, "For I am persuaded that neither death nor life, nor angels, nor principalities, nor things present, nor things to come, nor height, nor depth, nor any other thing created, shall be able to separate us from the love of God which is in Christ Jesus our Lord." We are eternally loved, connected, saved, empowered, healed, exalted, blessed, and forgiven. We are transformed by the divine power of God and we are eternally grateful to Jesus who is our Savior.

The End ....

ABOUT THE AUTHOR

Harriett Naomi Jones was born on August 12, 1983 to the late Rev. Clinton A. Jones and Allie Mae Lewis Jones of Homer, LA. She is the third of seven children and she has a host of nieces and nephews. She received her education at Homer Elementary School and Athens High School. She is also a proud Alumni of Grambling State University (Grambling, LA), graduating in 2005 with a B.A degree in Elementary Education. She is currently an Assistant Teacher at ABC Head start Center in Homer, LA. She is a faithful member of St. John Baptist Church.

Harriett's biggest passion is serving the Lord and helping and serving in her church and community. She credits God as being the center of her joy. As she stated, "I live and move because Jesus loves me and I love Him too. I am in the royal family of God and I can walk through any valley experience and come out on the winning side."

Harriett is the author of *10 Ways to Survive a Valley Experience*, a book that she knows will encourage people who are going through difficult times to see the light which is Jesus Christ.

www.ingramcontent.com/pod-product-compliance
Lightning Source LLC
Chambersburg PA
CBHW021125300426
44113CB00006B/295